LAWA'IH

A treatise on Sufism

Nur ud Din 'Abd ur Rahman Jami

Translated by
E.H Whinfield, M.A.,
& Mirza Muhammad
Kazvini

Qadeem Press

Qadeem Press

Qadeem Press Edition
Breathing Life into Forgotten Pages
www.qadeempress.com

Originally Published by Royal Asiatic Society in 1906
Reprinted by Qadeem Press in 2025

CONTENTS

PREFACE

The *Lawā'iḥ* is a treatise on Ṣūfī theology or theosophy, as distinguished from the religious emotions experienced by all Ṣūfīs, learned and unlearned alike. Catholic authorities have drawn this distinction between 'experimental' and 'doctrinal' mysticism,[1] and it is a great help towards clear thinking on this subject. The religious emotion common to all mankind is, so to speak, raised to its *n*th power in the mystics. They are overwhelmed by the sense of the Divine omnipresence, and of their own dependence on God. They are dominated and intoxicated by their vivid sense of the close relation subsisting between the soul and God. They conceive themselves as being in touch with God, feeling His motions in their souls, and at times rising to direct vision of Him by the 'inner light' vouchsafed to them. These religious experiences were the rough material out of which the doctrinal reasoned system, set out in treatises like the *Lawā'iḥ*, was built up. Psychologists have advanced various theories as to the genesis of these experiences.[2] With these we are not at present concerned. But as to the origin of the philosophical ideas and terms employed in the *Lawā'iḥ* and similar works to formulate the Ṣūfī theology, there can be little doubt. The source of Ṣūfī theology was Neoplatonism.

The title of the book, *Lawā'iḥ*, or 'Flashes of Light,'

[1] See the article on 'Mystical Theology' in Addis and Arnold's 'Catholic Dictionary.'

[2] See Dr. William James's 'Varieties of Religious Experience' (Longmans, 1902). It may be doubted whether the 'subliminal self' affords a satisfactory solution of the problem.

suggests the philosophy employed to systematize and give a reasoned basis for the unreasoned 'experiences' of unlearned Ṣūfīs. It of course refers to the 'inner light.' The Platonists were called *Ishrāqīn* or *Illuminati*, because they regarded intellectual intuition or intuitive reason as the main source of knowledge, whereas the Peripatetics (*Mashshā'īn*) recognised no sources of knowledge except the senses and the discursive reason (*Dianoia*). The word *Ishrāq*, or 'Lights,' is often met with in this connection. Thus Shams-ud-dīn Muḥammad ash-Shahrazūrī is called by Haji Khalfa 'a metaphysician learned in the inner lights' (*Ishrāq*).[1] Shihāb-ud-dīn as Suhrawardī, who was put to death at Aleppo in 537 A.H. by order of that valiant defender of the Faith, Sulṭān Ṣalāḥ-ud-dīn, wrote a book entitled *Ḥikmat-ul-Ishrāq*, or 'Philosophy of Inner Light.'[2] The author of the *Dabistān* says that the belief of the pure Ṣūfīs is the same as that of the *Ishrāqīn* or Platonists,[3] and also that Ṣūfīs were classed as orthodox (*Mutasharri'*) and Platonists.[4] Haji Khalfa, in his article on Ṣūfism (*Tasawwuf*), says that anyone who reads Ṣūfī books cannot fail to remark that their terminology is borrowed from the Platonists (*Ishrāqīn*), and more especially from the later ones—*i.e.*, the Neoplatonists.[5]

It was probably at about the end of the fifth century A.H. that Neoplatonic *gnōsis* began to influence and modify Ṣūfī doctrine. Up to that date the doctrine had been expounded in short precepts, parables (*mithāl*), and similes like those in the Koran. But educated Moslems had outgrown these primitive methods of instruction. They wanted something more systematic. Jalāl-ud-dīn Rūmī tells us how his critics assailed him for dealing in trivial examples and parables iustead of giving a systematic account of the stages of the soul's ascent to God.[6] Ibn Khaldūn mentions Muḥāsibī and

[1] Haji Khalfa, iii. 479.

[2] Ibn Khallikan, iv. 153. This Shihāb-ud-dīn must not be confounded with his more famous namesake who died at Baghdad in the odour of sanctity in 632 A.H. Ibn Khallikan, ii. 382.

[3] Shea and Troyer's translation, iii. 281.

[4] *Ibid.*, ii. 374 ; see also iii. 139.

[5] Haji Khalfa, ii. 308.

[6] See 'Masnavī,' p. 168.

the great Imām Ghazzālī as among the first who wrote systematic treatises on the doctrines of the Ṣūfīs.[1] We have Ghazzālī's own account of the way in which he was attracted to Ṣūfism,[2] and other passages in his writings prove that he used the forms of Greek thought to explain Ṣūfī principles.[3] If it be asked how Greek philosophy reached Ghazzālī, who was a native of Khurāsān,[4] the answer is easy. When Justinian closed the schools at Athens, Damascius and his Neoplatonist brethren fled to the court of Nushirvān. They only remained there about a year, and left in 533 A.D.; but Nushirvān had some translations of Neoplatonist books made at the time, and these were followed by many others, made two centuries and a half later, under the Abbasides at Baghdad.[5]

Greek philosophy was expounded by the so-called Arabian, but really Persian, philosophers, Al Farābī and Avicena, and afterwards in the *Ikhwān-us-Ṣafā*.[6] Shahrastānī, a contemporary of Ghazzālī, gave accounts of all the chief Greek philosophers, including the 'Shaikh of the Greeks' or Plotinus,[7] his editor Porphyry and Proklus. The so-called 'Theology of Aristotle,' which is a summary of the 'Enneads' of Plotinus,[8] appeared probably soon afterwards. The result was that Neoplatonism, mainly in the form expounded by Plotinus, was used by all the more learned Ṣūfīs to explain and justify the simple emotional sayings of the early Ṣūfīs. Henceforward, Neoplatonism pervades all systematic treatises on Ṣūfism, such as the *Faṣūṣ-ul-Ḥikam*, the *Maqṣad-ul-Aqṣā*,[9] the *Gulshan i Rāz*,[10] and the *Lawā'iḥ*. Even the poets use the

1 'Notices et Extraits des Manuscrits,' xii., pp. 301, 302.

2 See Schmölders, 'Écoles Philosophiques chez les Arabes,' p. 55.

3 See the passage on 'Tauḥīd' given in Appendix I.

4 Khurāsān was the 'focus of culture,' as Hammer says, and most of the philosophers came from that Eastern province.

5 Whittaker's 'Neoplatonists,' p. 133; and Schmölders, 'Documenta Philosophiæ Arabum' (Bonn, 1836), Introduction.

6 See Dieterici's 'Die Weltseele' (Leipzig, 1872).

7 See Haarbrücker's German translation of Shahrastānī's 'Book of Sects,' ii. 192 (Halle, 1850).

8 See Dr. Brönnle's note, *Journal of the Royal Asiatic Society*, April, 1901. The book was published with a Latin translation by Petrus Nicolaus in 1518.

9 The late Professor Palmer published a summary of this book under the title of 'Oriental Mysticism' (Cambridge, 1867).

10 Edited and translated by me (Trübner, 1880).

Greek terminology. Thus Ḥakīm Sanā'ī, who lived at the same time as Ghazzālī, introduces 'Universal Reason' and 'Universal Soul,' the second and third hypostases of the Trinity of Plotinus, and the principal later poets follow suit.[1]

The first Ṣūfīs differed from ordinary Moslems only in their quietism (*taslīm*) and their puritan ideal of life. They held the orthodox doctrines, with perhaps a few reservations. But when Greek influences came into play all these doctrines underwent more or less modification. Take the following samples:

1. The cardinal doctrine of Islām was altered from Monotheism to Monism. 'There is no God but Allah' became 'There is no real Being or real Agent but "The One," "The Truth"' (*Al Haqq*).

2. God is no longer a supramundane Deity, enthroned above the empyrean heaven, creating the world by one fiat, ruling His subjects, like some mighty monarch, by commands and prohibitions, and paying them wages according to their deserts. He has become a Being immanent and 'deeply interfused' in the universe,[2] and giving it all the real existence it has. The Koran speaks of Allah as omniscient, but omniscience was now expanded into 'omni-essence,' if one may use such a word.[3] And the Plotinian emanation doctrine was borrowed to support this.

3. Like all great religious teachers, Muḥammad laid chief stress on right conduct, and this consisted in implicit obedience to every one of Allah's commands, as disobedience to any one was sin. The distinction between moral laws and com-

[1] Mr. Nicholson has brought this out in his 'Dīwāni Shamsi Tabrīz' (Cambridge, 1898). For a sketch of the system of Plotinus see Appendix II.

[2] *Cp.* Wordsworth, 'Lines on Tintern Abbey':

'A sense sublime
Of something far more deeply interfused,
Whose dwelling is the light of setting suns,
And the round ocean and the living air,
And the blue sky, and in the heart of man;
A motion and a spirit that impels
All thinking things, all objects of all thought,
And rolls through all things.'

[3] 'Or omneity,' as Sir Thomas Browne calls it in the 'Religio Medici,' § 35.

mands merely relating to ritual observances was not clearly laid down. It has been said that Islām means 'striving after righteousness.'[1] That is so, but righteousness was interpreted as including the scrupulous observance of trivial rules as to ablutions, prayers, fasting, etc.[2] It may well be doubted if Muḥammad is responsible for some of the directions about ritual which are ascribed to him,[3] but, be this as it may, more and more importance came to be assigned to the scrupulous observance of these ritual forms. The early Ṣūfīs disliked this externalism, and came to regard all rites as of small account. They thought that the mechanical routine of rites (*taqlīd*) only served to induce the spiritual torpor, which Dante called 'Accidīa.'[4] St. Bernard remarked this result in his monks, but he set it down to the fault of the men, not to that of the system. The Ṣūfī theologians adopted the Neoplatonist view that the ritual law is not binding upon spiritual men. St. Paul held a similar view. Shabistarī contrasts the mere outward Islām of ritual observances with the true piety of some heathens, much to the advantage of the latter, and Jalāl-ud-dīn Rūmī declares that 'Fools exalt the Mosque while they ignore the true temple in the heart.'[5]

4. The Koranic doctrine of future rewards and punishments was ultimately refined away. The early Ṣūfīs held very strongly that love to God should be quite disinterested and untainted by hope of reward. They thought 'otherworldliness' no better than worldliness. According to the Ṣūfī theologians there is no material heaven or hell. When

[1] Surah, lxxii. 14; Hirschfeld, p. 14; and Suhrawardy's 'Sayings of Muḥammad.' Jorjānī defines Islām as unquestioning obedience and submission to Allah's commands ('Notices et Extraits des Manuscrits,' x., p. 53.

[2] See the rules about ablution, etc., in the 'Mishcāt ul Masābīḥ,' translated by Matthews (Calcutta, 1809). *Cp.* Omar Khayyām's 'whimsical complaint,' Quatrain 180.

[3] They seem opposed to the spirit of the text: 'Righteousness does not consist in turning to the east or to the west,' etc. (Surah, ii. 172).

[4] Purgatory (Canto XVII.).

[5] 'Gulshan i Rāz,' l. 877; and 'Masnavī,' p. 100, and Introduction, p. xxxiv (second edition). But elsewhere (at p. 76) Jalāl-ud-dīn says forms and symbols are generally needed. In default of some outward and visible sign which they can *per*ceive, men find it hard to *con*ceive the inward spirit.

union is attained, asked Shabistarī, 'of what account then will be Paradise and the Houris?'[1] On the other hand, those who lead evil lives would lose by degrees the portion of real being within them, dropping to the level of animals, or even plants, and finally relapsing into non-existence. This result is nowhere clearly stated, but seems implied in the language used, which is, of course, very guarded.[2]

5. Muḥammad had no taste for speculation. He said: 'Think on the mercies of God, not on the essence of God.' And again: 'Sit not with those who discuss predestination.' His language on predestination is merely popular. In one passage it is that of determinism, in another that of freewill. In one place Allah constrains all, guiding some aright and causing others to err.[3] Elsewhere man acts freely without constraint. But the theologians fastened on these obscure problems, and did their best to shift the religious centre of gravity from right conduct to right opinion on these problems. The traditionists fathered on Muḥammad various sayings to prove that he regarded orthodoxy on these 'afterthoughts of theology' as all important for salvation. Thus the saying, 'My people shall be split into seventy-three sects, all of whom but one shall perish in hell fire,' is one which betrays theological authorship. In Muḥammad's lifetime the contest was not with sects within Islām, but with those who denied Islām altogether. For these he had no mercy, but he would scarcely have been so hard on his own people for venial errors of opinion. Again, he could hardly have said, 'Qadarians are Magian (dualists),' at a time when (as is almost certain) no sect of that name had yet arisen.[4] The early Ṣūfīs did not concern themselves with the disputes of the sects. But the Ṣūfī theologians could not altogether ignore them. They took sides against the sects which leaned to anthropomorphism, and, on the other hand, fully agreed with the doctrine of the Compulsionists or extreme Predestinarians.[5] That sect held that God, as the One real Agent,

[1] 'Gulshan i Rāz,' l. 701.

[2] See Omar Khayyām (second edition), Appendix, p. 358.

[3] Koran, xvi. 38, 39.

[4] The Qadarians would be classed as semi-Pelagians by Western theologians.

[5] See 'Gulshan i Rāz,' l. 105 and 538.

not only permitted evil, but of set purpose allotted evils, present or future, to the majority of mankind. This strange doctrine (which has its parallel in Europe) forced the Ṣūfī theologians to attempt some reconciliation of Divine power, as thus interpreted, with Divine goodness, and here, like Augustine, they availed themselves of the 'not-being' (*'adm*) of Plotinus.[1]

Perhaps, however, the true Ṣūfī spirit was best interpreted by Jalāl-ud-dīn Rūmi, when he declared that he agreed with all seventy-three sects as being all honest attempts to grasp the obscure truth. Errors in 'naming the names of God' are of small account. According to the *Ḥadīth*, 'He who does the works will know the doctrine.' And true love to God atones for all mistakes of doctrine.[2]

Jāmī is a typical Ṣūfī theologian. He works hard to construct a reasoned basis for Ṣūfism, but finally realizes that his logical definitions and syllogisms cannot express the truth as it really is, and add nothing to the grounds on which the convictions of Ṣūfīs must always rest. It is only by means of the spiritual clairvoyance generated by love that Divine knowledge (*ma'rifat*) can be attained.[3] Those who have these spiritual intuitions do not need demonstrations, and to those who have them not all demonstrations are useless.

6. Muḥammad, like Luther, rejected asceticism. Suhrawardy quotes several of his anti-ascetic sayings, including the familiar one, 'There is no monasticism in Islām.' He approved of poverty, it is true, and prescribed a month of fasting, but set his face firmly against the cloistered life and celibacy.[4] The early Ṣūfīs were, perhaps, attracted to

[1] See 'Masnavī' (second edition), Introduction, p. xxx, etc., and Flash XXVII. in this treatise.

[2] See the parable of Moses and the shepherd who was faulty in theology, but fervent in spirit ('Masnavī,' p. 82, and also p. 139).

[3] See 'Masnavī,' p. 260. Newman ('Apologia,' p. 19) quotes Keble as saying, 'The firmness of assent which we give to religious doctrine is due, not to the probabilities which introduced it, but to the living power of faith and love which accepted it.' This is worked out in Newman's 'Grammar of Assent.'

[4] See the 'Sayings of Muḥammad,' by Suhrawardy (Constable, 1905), Nos. 125, 304, 186, etc.

asceticism by the example of the Christians in Syria, where the first Ṣūfī convent was built; and Neoplatonist doctrine furnished the rationale of ascetic practice. Matter was evil, and therefore all material and sensuous taint, including the natural instincts (*phronēma sarkos*), must be purged away and extirpated by all who claimed to be spiritual men.[1] Thus a double system of religious conduct was set up—the external law for ordinary men and 'the counsels of perfection,' the more perfect way of asceticism and contemplation for spiritual men. The external law of ritual observances had no longer any dominion over spiritual men.[2] This abrogation of the ceremonial law naturally tempted some undisciplined Ṣūfīs, as it has tempted some professing followers of St. Paul, to laxity in the observance of the moral law. It is needless to say that these antinomian developments were never countenanced by any reputable theologians or teachers, but, on the contrary, were always condemned by them. Still, it cannot be denied that wild enthusiasts and false brethren did occasionally misinterpret Ṣūfī doctrines in this way, and thus gave some ground for the prejudices of orthodox Moslems against the whole body of Ṣūfīs.

Harnack, in his 'History of Dogma,' has shown how profoundly Christian theology has been affected by Neoplatonist ideas. The disputes about *Ousia*, *Hypostasis*, and *Physis* which rent Christendom asunder[3] mainly grew from 'afterthoughts of theology' suggested by these ideas, and their influence has extended to our own days.[4] It is hardly too much to say that their influence on the course of events has been as considerable as that of the Roman law. In Islām their influence has been much more restricted than in Christendom, but, such as it was, it is instructive to trace it.[5]

[1] Jalāl-ud-dīn Rūmī, however, takes occasion to warn his disciples that this counsel of perfection is not to be taken too literally. See the parable of the peacock who tore off his plumage to avoid the pursuit of the fowlers ('Masnavī,' p. 228).

[2] See 'Masnavī,' p. 224.

[3] Gibbon's 'Decline and Fall,' chapter xxi.

[4] 'Paulus genuit Augustinum et Augustinus genuit Calvinum.' With Paul should be coupled Plotinus. See Bigg's 'Introduction to Augustine's Confessions' (Methuen, 1903).

[5] For a sketch of the system of Plotinus, who is the best exponent of Neoplatonism, see Appendix II.

The manuscript of the Lawā'iḥ now reproduced is undated, but was probably written within a century of Jāmī's death in 898 A.H. It once belonged to the royal library at Delhi, and the outside pages contain notes by the librarians, one of which, dated the twenty-fourth year of Aurangzīb, states that it was worm-eaten even then. W. H. Morley, who also owned it, has noted on the fly-leaf his opinion that it is not Jāmī's work, but written by one Sayyid ' Abd-ul Kāfi. This, however, is certainly a mistake. Haji Khalfa, in his notice of Jāmī's *Lawā'iḥ*, quotes the beginning, which agrees with the beginning of this manuscript,[1] and one of the quatrains gives Jāmī's name. The British Museum possesses three copies—viz., Add. 16,820 (Rieu, p. 44*a*); Add. 16,819, iv (Rieu, p. 826*b*); and Add. 7,689, iv, folio 150 onwards (Rieu, p. 810*b*). Copies are to be found in other libraries. In addition to that now reproduced, I possess one, written in an Indian hand, probably in the eighteenth century.[2]

The facsimile of the manuscript has been made by Messrs. Nops, of Ludgate Hill. They have been very successful in removing nearly all traces of the stains and worm-holes in the original, and I think the writer of the manuscript himself, could he see it, would find little fault with their reproduction of his handiwork.

I began the translation some years ago, but, owing to failing eyesight, had to stop after getting to the end of Flash VII. I have now been fortunate enough to secure the assistance of a very competent scholar, Mīrzā Muḥammad Ḳazvīnī, who has furnished me with a literal French version of the whole, together with some valuable notes. In his translation the Mīrzā has chiefly followed the British Museum Manuscript, Add. No. 16,819, which contains several passages not found in this manuscript. Most, if not all, of these seem to me to be glosses which have crept into the text, but I have given them in this translation, marking them with square brackets. Up to the end of Flash VII. the accompanying translation is that made by me some years ago, with some corrections sug-

[1] Haji Khalfa, v. 344.

[2] The Munich 'Catalogue,' p. 21, mentions a manuscript of the 'Lawāyih' (*sic*) with a different beginning.

gested by the Mīrzā's version. From the beginning of Flash VIII. to the end of the book the translation is the Mirza's French version turned into English by me. In this part of the work I have followed the Mīrzā closely, only referring to the original to verify a word here and there. I am solely responsible for the preface and notes. If they contain errors of fact or doctrine, these must not be imputed to the Mīrzā.

The references to the *Gulshan i Rāz* are to my edition of that work (Trübner, 1880); those to the *Masnavī* of Jalāl-ud-dīn Rūmī to my translation of that poem (second edition, published in Trübner's Oriental Series, 1898); those to Omar Khayyām to my text and translation, published in the same series, second edition, 1901.

As regards transliteration, I follow the rule laid down long since by the Indian Government, that when foreign words have become naturalized in English they should be spelled according to English usage. Thus I write Calcutta, Delhi, Koran, Abbasides, etc. Again, when a Persian writer has chosen to transliterate his own name in a particular way, I do not presume to interfere with his discretion. I give titles of books as they are spelled on the title-pages, and, like Rieu, I represent *Hamza* by the 'spiritus lenis' ('). With these exceptions I have in the main observed the transliteration rules of the Royal Asiatic Society.

E. H. W.

TRANSLATION OF THE LAWA'IH.

'I do not render praises unto Thee.'[1] How is this, seeing that 'all praise returns to Thee'?[2] The threshold of Thy sanctity is too high for my praises. Thou art what Thine own praises declare Thee. O Lord, we are not able to tell Thy praises or set forth Thy glories. Whatsoever is manifested on the pages of the universe is praise reflected back to the threshold of Thy most glorious Majesty. What can faculty or tongue of mine declare worthy of Thy glory and honour? Thou art such as Thou hast Thyself declared, and the pearls of Thy praise are what Thyself hast strung.

> In the vast largesse of Thy Majesty
> This whole world's but a drop from out the sea;
> What power have we to celebrate Thy praise?
> No praises save Thine own are meet for Thee!

Where the speaker of the words, 'I am the most eloquent [of the Arabs'],[3] lowered the flag of his eloquence, and found himself impotent to render Thee fitting praises, how shall a mere stammerer venture to open his mouth or a dullard deliver an apt discourse? Nevertheless, in this case to excuse one's self on the ground of one's incapacity and deficiencies is itself the gravest of defects, and to put one's self on a level with that prince of the world and of the faith would be a serious breach of propriety.

[1] A saying of Muḥammad.

[2] Fluegel (Haji Khalfa, v. 344) translates, 'Quomodo possim?' *Cp.* Surah, xvii. 46, 'Neither is there aught which doth not celebrate Thy praise,' and Ps. cxlv. 10.

[3] Referring to the saying, 'I am the most eloquent of those who pronounce the letter Zād (Dzād),' the Arab shibboleth.

What am I? Can I count myself the peer
Of the poor dog that's suffered to draw near?
I may not join the caravan—enough
If from afar the camel bells I hear.

O Lord, send down Thy blessing upon Muḥammad, the standard-bearer of praise and possessor of 'the glorious station,'[1] and upon his family, and upon his companions who through earnest endeavour have succeeded in attaining the goal of their desire, and pour upon them all Thy perfect peace!

SUPPLICATIONS.[2]

O God, deliver us from preoccupation with worldly vanities, and show us the nature of things 'as they really are.'[3] Remove from our eyes the veil of ignorance, and show us things as they really are. Show not to us non-existence as existent, nor cast the veil of non-existence over the beauty of existence. Make this phenomenal world the mirror[4] to reflect the manifestations of Thy beauty, and not a veil to separate and repel us from Thee. Cause these unreal phenomena of the universe to be for us the sources of knowledge and insight, and not the cause of ignorance and blindness. Our alienation and severance from Thy beauty all proceed from ourselves. Deliver us from ourselves, and accord to us intimate knowledge of Thee.

Make my heart pure, my soul from error free,
Make tears and sighs my daily lot to be,
And lead me on Thy road away from self,
That lost to self I may approach to Thee!

Set enmity between the world and me,
Make me averse from worldly company:
From other objects turn away my heart,
So that it be engrossed with love to Thee.

[1] 'It may be, O Muḥammad, that thy Lord will raise thee to a glorious station' (Koran, xvii. 81), interpreted to mean, his power of intercession.

[2] The headings are all omitted in this manuscript, but spaces are left, which were probably intended to be filled in with gold lettering.

[3] A prayer ascribed to Muḥammad. See 'Gulshan i Rāz,' p. 21, note 1.

[4] The divine Real Being is reflected in 'Notbeing' (*'adm*) as in a mirror, and gives it all the reality it possesses. See 'Gulshan i Rāz,' p. 14, l. 134. This idea comes from Plotinus, 'the Shaikh of the Greeks.'

How were it, Lord, if Thou should'st set me free
From error's grasp and cause me truth to see?
  Guebres by scores Thou makest Musulmans,
Why, then, not make a Musulman of me?

My lust for this world and the next efface,
Grant me the crown of poverty and grace
  To be partaker in Thy mysteries,
From paths that lead not towards Thee turn my face.

PREFACE.

This is a treatise entitled *Lawa'iḥ*[1] ('Flashes of Light'), explanatory of the intuitions and verities displayed on the pages of the hearts and minds of men of insight and divine knowledge, and of those who enjoy spiritual raptures and ecstasies. It is written in suitable language adorned with pleasing explanations. I trust that readers will hold of no account the personality of the author of this commentary, and will refrain from taking their seats upon the carpet of cavilling and animadversion. For the author plays only the part of interpreter in the following discussions; his sole function is that of mouthpiece, and nothing else.

Believe me, I am naught—yea, less than naught.
By naught and less than naught what can be taught?
  I tell the mysteries of truth, but know
Naught save the telling to this task I brought.

For poverty to make no sign is best,
On love divine to hold one's peace is best;
  For him who never felt ecstatic joys
To play a mere reporter's part is best.

With men of light I sought these pearls to string,
The drift of mystics' sayings forth to bring;
  Now let his trusty slaves this tribute bear
From foolish me to Hamadān's wise king.'[2]

[1] Haji Khalfa (v., p. 344) says Sayyid Kāseh Karrānī wrote a Persian commentary upon it.

[2] The person referred to is probably Shāh Manuchahr, Governor of Hamadān, who paid much attention to Jāmī when he visited the town in 877 A.H. See Lee's preface to the 'Nafaḥāt,' p. 11. Note the pun on 'Hama Dān' ('All-knowing'). Amīr Sayyid 'Alī of Hamadan, a Ṣūfī saint, is mentioned in the 'Nafaḥāt,' p. 515, but as he died in 786 A.H., it is not likely that Jāmī is speaking of him.

Flash I.[1]

God has not made man with two hearts within him.[2] The Incomparable Majesty who has conferred the boon of existence upon thee has placed within thee but one heart, to the end that with single heart thou mayest love Him alone, and mayest turn thy back on all besides and devote thyself to Him alone, and refrain from dividing thy heart into a hundred portions, each portion devoted to a different object.

O votary of earthly idols' fane,
Why let these veils of flesh enwrap thy brain?
'Tis folly to pursue a host of loves;
A single heart can but one love contain!

Flash II.

Distraction or disunion (*Tafriqah*) consists in dividing the heart by attaching it to divers objects. Union or collectedness (*jam'iyyat*[3]) consists in forsaking all else and being wholly engrossed in the contemplation of the One Unique Being. Those who fancy that collectedness results from the collecting of worldly goods remain in perpetual distraction, whilst those who are convinced that amassing wealth is the cause of distraction renounce all worldly goods.

O thou whose heart is torn by lust for all,
Yet vainly strives to burst these bonds of all,
This 'all' begets distraction of the heart:
Give up thy heart to ONE and break with all.

While thou'rt distraught by hell-born vanity,
Thou'rt seen by men of union base to be;
By God, thou art a demon,[4] and no man,
Too ignorant thy devilry to see.

O pilgrim[5] on the 'path' vain talk reject;
All roads save that to Unity neglect;
Naught but distractedness proceeds from wealth:
Collect thine heart, not store of wealth collect.

[1] 'Lā'iḥah.' These headings, which are found in other manuscripts, are omitted in this, as before remarked.
[2] Koran, xxxiii. 4.
[3] Also 'tranquillity,' 'congregation,' 'totality.'
[4] *Nasnās*; literally, a fabulous monster, a satyr.
[5] *Sālik*.

O heart, thy high-prized learning of the schools,
Geometry and metaphysic rules—
Yea, all but lore of God is devils' lore :
Fear God and leave this evil lore to fools.

Flash III.

The 'Truth,' most glorious and most exalted, is omnipresent. He knows the outer and inner state of all men in every condition. Oh, what a loss will be thine if thou turnest thine eyes from His face to fix them on other objects, and forsakest the way that is pleasing to Him to follow other roads!

My Love stood by me at the dawn of day,
And said, 'To grief you make my heart a prey;
Whilst I am casting looks of love at you,
Have you no shame to turn your eyes away?'

All my life long I tread love's path of pain,
If peradventure 'union' I may gain.
Better to catch one moment's glimpse of Thee
Than earthly beauties' love through life retain.

Flash IV.

Everything other than the 'Truth' (may He be glorified and exalted) is subject to decay and annihilation. Its substance is a mental figment with no objective existence, and its form is a merely imaginary entity.

Yesterday this universe neither existed nor appeared to exist, while to-day it appears to exist, but has no real existence: it is a mere semblance, and to-morrow nothing thereof will be seen. What does it profit thee to allow thyself to be guided by vain passions and desires? Why dost thou place reliance on these transitory objects that glitter with false lustre? Turn thy heart away from all of them, and firmly attach it to God. Break loose from all these, and cleave closely to Him. It is only He who always has been and always will continue to be. The countenance of His eternity is never scarred by the thorn of contingency.

The fleeting phantoms you admire to-day
Will soon at Heaven's behest be swept away.
O give your heart to Him who never fails,
Who's ever with you and will ever stay.

When to fair idols' shrines I did repair,
I vexed my heart with griefs encountered there ;
Now earthly beauty has lost all its charm,
Eternal beauty is my only care.

Things that abide not to eternity
Expose thee to misfortune's battery ;
In *this* life, then, sever thyself from all
From which thy death is bound to sever thee.

Perchance with wealth and sons endowed thou art.
Yet with all these erelong thou'lt have to part.
Thrice happy he who gives his heart to ONE,
And sets affection on the men of heart.

Flash V.

The Absolute Beauty is the Divine Majesty endued with [the attributes of] power and bounty. Every beauty and perfection manifested in the theatre of the various grades of beings is a ray of His perfect beauty reflected therein. It is from these rays that exalted souls have received their impress of beauty and their quality of perfection.[1] Whosoever is wise derives his wisdom from the Divine wisdom. Wherever intelligence is found it is the fruit of the Divine intelligence. In a word, all are attributes of Deity which have descended from the zenith of the Universal and Absolute to the nadir of the particular and relative. [They have descended] to the end that thou mayest direct thy course from the part towards the Whole, and from the relative deduce the Absolute, and not imagine the part to be distinct from the Whole, nor be so engrossed with what is merely relative as to cut thyself off from the Absolute.

The Loved One's rose-parterre I went to see,
That beauty's Torch[2] espied me, and, quoth He,
'I am the tree ; these flowers My offshoots are.
Let not these offshoots hide from thee the tree.'

[1] Spenser in the 'Hymn of Heavenly Love' expresses the same idea, which comes from Plato.

[2] Literally, 'Torch of Tirāz,' a town in Turkistān famed for its beautiful women.

What profit rosy cheeks, forms full of grace,
And ringlets clustering round a lovely face?
When Beauty Absolute beams all around,
Why linger finite beauties to embrace?

Flash VI.

Man, in regard to his corporeal nature, stands at the lowest point of degradation; nevertheless, in regard to his spiritual nature, he is at the summit of nobility. He takes the impress of every thing to which he directs his attention, and assumes the colour of every thing to which he approaches. Wherefore philosophers say that when the reasonable soul adorns itself with exact and faithful impressions of realities, and appropriates to itself the true character of such realities, it becomes such as if it were itself altogether essential Being. In like manner the vulgar, by the force of their conjunction with these material forms and extreme preoccupation with these corporeal liens, come to be such that they cannot distinguish themselves from these forms or perceive any difference between the two. Well says the Maulavī of Rūm (may God sanctify his secret) in the *Masnavī*:

O brother, thou art wholly thought,
For the rest of thee is only bone and muscle:
If thy thought be a rose, thou art a rose-bouquet;
If it be a thorn, thou art fuel for the fire.

Wherefore it behoves thee to strive and hide thy*self* from thy sight,[1] and occupy thyself with Very Being, and concern thyself with the 'Truth.' For the various grades of created things are theatres of His revealed beauty, and all things that exist are mirrors of his perfections.

And in this course thou must persevere until He mingles Himself with thy soul, and thine own individual existence passes out of thy sight. Then, if thou regardest thyself, it is He whom thou art regarding; if thou speakest of thyself, it is He of whom thou art speaking. The relative has become the Absolute, and 'I am the Truth' is equivalent to 'He is the Truth.'[2]

[1] Variant, 'hide thyself from the sight of the world.'
[2] The saying of Manṣūr i Ḥallāj (or Ibn Ḥallāj), the Ṣūfī martyr.

If love of rose or bulbul fill thine heart,
Thyself a rose or eager bulbul art.
  Thou art a part; the 'Truth' is all in all.
Dwell on the 'Truth,' and cease to be a part.

Of my soul's union with this fleshly frame,
Of life and death Thou art the end and aim.
  I pass away; Thou only dost endure.
When I say 'me,' 'tis Thee I mean to name.[1]

When will this mortal dress be torn away,
And Beauty Absolute His face display,
  Merging my soul in His resplendent light,
Blinding my heart with His o'erpowering ray?

Flash VII.

It is necessary for thee to habituate thyself to this intimate relation in such wise that at no time and in no circumstance thou mayest be without the sense of it, whether in coming or in going, in eating or sleeping, in speaking or listening. In short, thou must ever be on the alert both when resting and when working, not to waste thy time in insensibility [to this relation]—nay, more, thou must watch every breath, and take heed that it goeth not forth in negligence.

The years roll on; Thou showest not Thy face,
Yet nothing from my breast Thy love can chase;
  Thine image ever dwells before mine eyes,
And in my heart Thy love aye holds its place.

Flash VIII.

In like manner, as it behoves thee to maintain the said relation continually, so it is of the first importance to develop the quality thereof by detaching thyself from mundane relations and by emancipating thyself from attention to contingent forms; and this is possible only through hard striving and earnest endeavour to expel vain thoughts and imaginations from thy mind. The more these thoughts are cast out and

[1] Compare the story of the Ṣūfī aspirant who was refused admittance by his Pīr till he ceased to speak of 'me' and called himself 'thee' ('Masnavī,' p. 47).

these suggestions checked, the stronger and closer this relation becomes. It is, then, necessary to use every endeavour to force these thoughts to encamp outside the enclosure of thy breast, and that the 'Truth' most glorious may cast His beams into thy heart, and deliver thee from thyself, and save thee from the trouble of entertaining His rivals in thy heart. Then there will abide with thee neither consciousness of thyself, nor even consciousness of such absence of consciousness[1]—nay, there will abide nothing save the One God alone.

From my brute nature,[2] Lord, deliver me,
And from this life of evil set me free;
Purge me of my own sense and ignorance,
And make me lose my very self in Thee.

When poor indeed and dead to self thou'lt need
No visions, knowledge, certitude, or creed;
When self has perished naught but God remains,
For 'Perfect poverty is God indeed.'[3]

Flash IX.

Self-annihilation consists in this, that through the overpowering influence of the Very Being upon the inner man, there remains no consciousness of aught beside Him. Annihilation of annihilation consists in this, that there remains no consciousness even of that unconsciousness. It is evident that annihilation of annihilation is involved in [the very notion of] annihilation. For if he who has attained annihilation should retain the least consciousness of his annihilation, he would not be in the state of annihilation, because the quality of annihilation and the person possessing such quality are both things distinct from the Very Being, the 'Truth' most glorious. Therefore, to be conscious of annihilation is incompatible with annihilation.[4]

[1] See the passage from Ghazzālī in Appendix III.
[2] *Dadī*, brutishness. Some manuscripts read *duwī*, disease, but this does not suit the rhyme, which in verses with a burden (*radīf*) always precedes it. Scan *dădīyi*, dissolving long ī and lengthening the *iẓāfat*.
[3] Seemingly a Ḥadīth. Poverty, utter annihilation of self ('Gulshan i Rāz,' l. 128, and note).
[4] So Ghazzālī, quoted in Appendix III.

While fondness for your 'self' you still retain,
You'll not reduce its bulk a single grain—
  Yea, while you feel one hair's-breadth of yourself
Claims to annihilation are but vain.

Flash X.

Unification[1] consists in unifying the heart—that is to say, in purifying it and expelling from it attachment to all things other than the 'Truth' most glorious, including not only desire and will, but also knowledge and intelligence. In fact, one must quench desire of all things hitherto desired, and cease to will what one has hitherto willed, and also remove from the intellectual vision all concepts and all cognitions, and turn away the mind from all things whatsoever, so that there remains no consciousness or cognition of aught save the 'Truth' most glorious. [Khwāja 'Abdullāh Anṣārī said: 'Unification is not merely believing Him to be One, but in thyself being one with Him.'[2]

'Oneness' in pilgrims' phraseology
Is from concern with 'other' to be free;
  Learn, then, the highest 'station' of the birds,[3]
If language of the birds be known to thee.'

Flash XI.

So long as a man remains imprisoned in the snare of passions and lusts, it is hard for him to maintain this close communion [with the 'Truth']. But from the moment that sweet influence takes effect on him, expelling from his mind the firebrand of vain imaginations and suggestions, the pleasure he experiences therefrom predominates over bodily pleasures and intellectual enjoyments. Then the painful sense of effort passes away, and the joys of contemplation

[1] *Tauḥīd* is the *Henōsis* of Plotinus, the becoming one with the 'One.'

[2] This sentence occurs only in the British Museum copy, Add. 16,819. Khwāja 'Abdullāh Anṣārī of Herāt, who died 481 A.H., was named the Shaikh of Islām, and is often quoted by Jāmī in the 'Nafaḥāt.' See Haji Khalfa, i., 235.

[3] Alluding to the 'Discourse of the Birds and their Pilgrimage to the Sīmurgh,' by Farīd-ud-dīn 'Aṭṭār. 'Other' the *Heterotēs* of Plotinus.

take possession of his mind; he banishes from his heart all alien distractions, and with the tongue of ecstasy murmurs this canticle:

Like bulbul I'm inebriate with Thee,[1]
My sorrows grow from memories of Thee,
  Yet all earth's joys are dust beneath the feet
Of those entrancing memories of Thee.

Flash XII.

When the true aspirant perceives in himself the beginnings of this Divine attraction, which consists in experiencing pleasure whenever he thinks of the 'Truth' most glorious, he ought to exert all his endeavours to develop and strengthen this experience, and simultaneously to banish whatever is incompatible therewith. He ought to know, for instance, that even though he should employ an eternity in cultivating this communion, that would count as nothing, and he would not have discharged his duty as he ought.

On my soul's lute a chord was struck by Love,
Transmuting all my being into love;
  Ages would not discharge my bounden debt
Of gratitude for one short hour of love.

Flash XIII.

The essence of the 'Truth' most glorious and most exalted is nothing but Being. His[2] Being is not subject to defect or diminution. He is untouched by change or variation, and is exempt from plurality and multiplicity; He transcends all manifestations, and is unknowable and invisible. Every 'how' and 'why' have made their appearance through Him; but in Himself He transcends every 'how' and 'why.' Everything is perceived by Him, while he is beyond perception. The out-

[1] So in the *Stabat Mater*:

'Fac me cruce inebriari.'

[2] I prefer to emphasize the religious rather than the philosophic and abstract aspect of the 'Truth,' and therefore use the personal pronoun. Thus, the 'Ideal Good' of Plato's 'Republic,' Book VI., is spoken of as 'God' in the 'Timæus.' Just so 'To Kurion' has changed into 'Dominus' in the Western version of the Nicene Creed.

ward eye is too dull to behold His beauty, and the eye of the heart is dimmed by the contemplation of His perfection.

Thou, for whose love I've sacrificed existence,
Art, yet art not, the sum of earth's existence;
Earth lacks true Being, yet depends thereon—
Thou art true Being: Thou art pure existence.

The Loved One is quite colourless,[1] O heart;
Be not engrossed with colours, then, O heart:
All colours come from what is colourless,
And 'who can dye so well as God,'[2] O heart?

Flash XIV.

By the word 'existence'[3] is sometimes meant simply the state of being or existing, which is a generic concept or an abstract idea. Taken in this sense, 'existence' is an 'idea of the second intention,'[4] which has no external object corresponding with it. It is one of the accidents of the 'quidity'[5] [or real nature of the thing] which exists only in thought, as has been proved by the reasonings of scholastic theologians and philosophers. But sometimes 'existence' signifies the Real Being, who is Self-existent, and on whom the existence of all other beings depends; and in truth there is no real external existence beside Him—all other beings are merely accidents accessory to Him, as is attested by the intuitive apprehension of the most famous Gnostics and 'Men of Certitude.' The word ['existence'] is applicable to the 'Truth' most glorious in the latter sense only.

Things that exist to men of narrow view
Appear the accidents to substance due;
To men of light substance is accident,
Which the 'True Being' ever doth renew.[6]

[1] Bīrangī. Absence of visible or knowable qualities.
[2] Koran, ii. 132.
[3] *Wajūd*, usually 'necessary being' as opposed to 'contingent.' Jāmī wrote a treatise on it, quoted in the 'Dabistān,' chapter xii.
[4] *Ma'qūlāt i thānīyah.* In scholastic terminology terms of the second intention are those which express abstractions from concrete individual objects—*e.g.*, genus, species, etc. Rabelais made fun of this term: 'Utrum chimæra bombinans in vacuo comedere possit secundas intentiones?'
[5] Quidity, what a thing is, a word derived by the Schoolmen from *māhīyat.* See Schmölders, 'Documenta Philosophiæ Arabum,' p. 133.
[6] 'In Him we live and move and have our being' (Acts xvii. 28).

Flash XV.

The attributes are distinct from the Real Being in thought, but are identical with Him in fact and reality. For instance, the Real Being is omniscient in respect of His quality of knowledge; omnipotent in respect of His power; absolute in respect of His will. Doubtless, just as these attributes are distinct from each other in idea, according to their respective meanings, so they are distinct from the Real Being; but in fact and reality they are identical with Him. In other words, there are not in Him many existences, but only one sole existence, and His various names and attributes are merely His modes and aspects

Pure is Thy essence from deficiency,
Expressed its 'how' and 'where' can never be;
Thy attributes appear distinct, but are
One with Thy essence in reality.

Flash XVI.

The Real Being, *quâ* Being, is above all names and attributes, and exempt from all conditions and relations. The attribution to Him of these names only holds good in respect of His aspect towards the world of phenomena. In the first manifestation, wherein He revealed Himself, of Himself, to Himself, were realized the attributes of Knowledge, Light, Existence and Presence. Knowledge involved the power of knowing and that of being known; Light implied those of manifesting and of being manifest; Existence and Presence entailed those of causing to exist and of being existent, and those of beholding and of being beheld. And thus the manifestation which is a characteristic of Light is preceded by concealment; and concealment, by its very nature, has the priority over, and is antecedent to, manifestation; hence the concealed and the manifested are counted as first and second.

And in like manner in the case of the second and third manifestations, etc., as long as it pleases God to continue them, these conditions and relations always go on redoubling themselves. The more these are multiplied, the more complete is His manifestation, or rather His concealment. Glory be to Him who hides Himself by the manifestations of His light, and manifests Himself by drawing a veil over His face. His concealment has regard to His pure and absolute Being, while His manifestation has regard to the exhibition of the world of phenomena.

'O fairest rose,[1] with rosebud mouth,' I sighed,
'Why, like coquettes, thy face for ever hide?'
He smiled, 'Unlike the beauties of the earth,
Even when veiled I still may be descried.'

Thy face uncovered would be all too bright,
Without a veil none could endure the sight;
What eye is strong enough to gaze upon
The dazzling splendour of the fount of light?

When the sun's banner blazes in the sky,
Its light gives pain by its intensity,
But when 'tis tempered by a veil of cloud
That light is soft and pleasant to the eye.

Flash XVII.

The first Epiphany[2] is a pure unity and a simple potentiality, which contains all potentialities, including not only that of being unconditioned by modes and qualities, but also that of being conditioned thereby. Viewed as unconditioned by modes and qualities, including even the potentiality of being thus unconditioned, it is the stage termed 'Unity'; and so possesses Concealment, Priority, and Existence from eternity. On the other hand, when viewed as conditioned by modes and qualities, it is the stage termed 'Singleness,' and in this aspect it is marked by Manifestation, Posteriority, and Duration to all eternity. Among these modes of the stage 'Singleness,' some are such that the qualification of the One

[1] *Cp.* 'Rosa mystica' in the Litany of the Virgin. Jalāl-ud-dīn Rūmī apologizes for applying such terms to God ('Masnavī,' p. 34).

[2] *Ta'ayyun.* The first Emmanation is 'Unity' with the 'Truth' as being His image and mind (*Logos endiathetos*), but when evolved to view (*Logos prophorikos*), and as the channel of Being downwards, it is 'Unity' with a difference, which is sought to be expressed by the term 'Singleness' (*Wāḥidīyat* instead of *Aḥadīyat*).

Being by them has regard to the stage called the 'Whole,'[1] whether they imply the realization in the universe of things corresponding to the names 'Creator' and 'Sustainer,' etc., or merely attributes, such as Life, Knowledge, and Will. This is the class of attributes which pertain to the Divinity and the Sovereignty. The forms under which the One Real Being is conceived, when clothed with these names and attributes, are the 'divine substances.'[2] The clothing of the outward aspect of Being[3] with these forms does not necessitate multiplicity of beings. Other modes are such that the qualification of the One Real Being by them has relation to the various grades of 'mundane existences,'[4] as, for instance, Difference, Property,[5] and the phenomena which distinguish external objects from one another. The forms under which the One Real Being is conceived, when clothed with these modes, are 'the mundane substances,'[6] and the clothing of the outward aspect of Being with these forms *does* necessitate a multiplicity of beings. Among these mundane substances, some are such that when Being, considered in the stage of the 'Unity of the Whole,'[7] is interfused in them, and His effects and properties manifest themselves therein, these substances have the potentiality of being theatres exhibiting *all* the Divine names—save those peculiar to the Divine Essence—according to the varying strength of the manifestations, which may be powerful or feeble, irresistible or defeasible. These are the perfect individuals of the human race—to wit, prophets and saints. Others, again, are such that they have the potentiality of being theatres exhibiting only some of the

[1] *Martaba i Jam'*. The second emanation, Universal Soul, which comprehends in itself all particular souls, rational, animal, and vegetive. This Aristotelian doctrine of the soul became a commonplace of the schools, and is referred to by Milton, Dryden, etc.

[2] Substance is *quod substat—i.e.*, the reality underlying sensible phenomena. *Ḥaqāiq i ilāhīya*.

[3] *I.e.*, the first stage of His revelation.

[4] *Marātib i kaunīya*.

[5] Difference, property, accident, genus, and species, are the five heads under which Aristotle classed the general terms capable of being used as predicates.

[6] *Ḥaqāiq i kaunīya*.

[7] *Āḥadīyat i Jam'*. This is the second emanation (see Flash XXIV.). It is usually called *nafs i kull*, or Universal Soul.

Divine names, and not all of them, according to the aforesaid varying strength of the manifestation. These are the rest of the human race.

The Majesty of the One Real Being, viewed under the aspect of the 'Unity of the Whole,' which comprehends all His modes, both Divine and mundane,[1] is for ever immanent in all these substances, and manifesting Himself in them. These substances are the parts of the whole Unity, whether they exist in the world of spirits or in that of 'ideas,'[2] in the sensible and visible world, in the world that now is, or in that which is to come. The final Cause[3] of all this process is the realization or manifestation of the perfection of the Divine names, which is termed *jalā* and *istijlā*. *Jalā* signifies their outward manifestation according to their various modes; and *istijlā* their display to the Deity Himself, according to these same modes. *Jalā* is a visible and intelligible manifestation or representation, just as the whole is represented by its parts. Contrariwise, the perfection of the Divine Essence, is the manifestation of the One Real Being to Himself, for Himself, without relation to anything beside Himself. This is a secret and intelligible manifestation.

Absolute self-sufficiency is a quality involved in Divine Perfection. It signifies this, that in a general and universal manner all the modes, states, and aspects of the One Real Being with all their adherent properties and qualities, in all their presentations, past, present or future, manifested in all grades of substances, Divine and mundane, are present and realized in the secret thought of that Divine Being, in such wise that the sum of them all is contained in His Unity. From this point of view He is independent of all other existences, as it is said, 'God most glorious can do without the world':[4]

[1] *I.e.*, plurality summed up in Unity.

[2] The world of 'ideas' is the Platonic 'intelligible' world of ideas or archetypes, apprehended only by Reason (*nous*), as opposed to the 'sensible' world of phenomena apprehended by the senses—'*ālam i 'ilmī* as opposed to '*ālam i 'ainī*.

[3] In Aristotle's language the end (*telos*) of a thing is its 'final cause'—*i.e.*, the reason of its existence.

[4] Koran, xxix. 5.

The robe of Love is independent, free
From need to soil with dust its purity;
  When Actor and Spectator are the same
What means this 'we' and 'thou'? There is
    no 'we.'[1]

All modes and attributes of Very Being
Are realized and present in that Being;
  To see them He needs not contingent beings:[2]
'Tis the contingent needs the Very Being.

He needs not to see good and ill set out,
The One needs not to count its numbers out;[3]
  The Truth can view all things within Himself;
What need, then, to review them all without?

Flash XVIII.

When you abstract the appearances and characteristics of the individuals which constitute the various species included in the genus 'animal,'[4] the individuals are gathered up into their respective species. When, again, you abstract the characteristics of each species, *i.e.*, their 'differences' and 'properties,' all such species are gathered up into the reality of the genus 'animal.' Again, when you abstract the characteristics of the genus 'animal,' and those of all other genera included in the higher genus 'growing body,' all such genera coalesce under that genus, 'growing body.' So when you abstract the characteristics of 'growing body,' and all other genera included along with it under the higher genus 'body,' all such genera are united in the reality of the genus 'body.' Furthermore, when you abstract the characteristics of 'body' and those of all other genera included therewith in

[1] *Cp.* Omar Khayyām, Quatrain 475, and 'Gulshan i Rāz,' p. 15, l. 143. 'He [God] is at once seer and thing seen.'

[2] Contingent being is opposed to necessary being. It is, so to speak, unreal matter permeated with Real Being. 'It thus is, and is not, and partakes both of existence and of non-existence,' as Jowett says.

[3] So Manṣur-i-Ḥallāj: 'The numbers of Unity are only the counting of Unity.'

[4] The controversy of realism and nominalism raged among Moslems as well as among European Schoolmen (see Schmölders, 'Documenta,' etc., p. 3). Jāmī was evidently a realist. He holds genus and similar general terms to be actual realities (*ma'nī*), and not mere names. The whole argument in this section rests on the assumption that these genera are real entities.

the higher genus 'substance,' to wit, the 'intelligences' and 'souls,' all such genera will be united in the reality of the higher genus 'substance'; so when you abstract the characteristics distinctive of 'substance' and 'accident,' these two genera are united into the [reality of the genus] 'contingent.' Finally, when you abstract the characteristic distinctions of 'contingent' and 'necessary,' these two are united in the 'Absolute Existence,' which is the veritable Being, existing of Himself, and not through another being beyond Himself. Necessity is His external quality, and 'Contingency' His internal quality—*i.e.*, they are the 'archetypal ideas'[1] generated by His self-revelation to Himself when assuming His 'modes.'

All these distinctions, whether called 'difference' and 'property' or 'appearances' and 'characteristics,' are 'Divine Modes,' contained and involved in the 'Unity of the One Real Being.' First, these modes are represented under the form of the 'archetypal ideas' in the stage called the 'Divine Thought' (or knowledge);[2] in the next place, in the stage of the 'sensible world,' when clothed with the properties and attributes of external existence—which is the theatre of manifestation, a mirror reflecting the inner Divine Being—these modes assume the forms of external objects.

It follows, therefore, that in the external world there is only One Real Being, who, by clothing Himself with different modes and attributes, appears to be endued with multiplicity and plurality to those who are confined in the narrow prison of the 'stages,' and whose view is limited to visible properties and results.

Creation's book I studied from my youth,
And every page examined, but in sooth
I never found therein aught save the 'Truth,'
And attributes that appertain to 'Truth.'

[1] *A'yān i thābitah,* the 'Ideas' of Plato's 'Intelligible World,' the archetypes or patterns of all things in the external and 'sensible world.' In the system of Plotinus these ideas are all contained in the first emanation, reason (*nous*). Jāmī expresses 'intelligible world' by *'ālam i 'ilm,* and 'sensible world' by *'ālam i 'ain.*

[2] *Martaba i 'ilm, i.e., 'aql i kull, nous,* or *Logos,* the first epiphany or emanation.

What mean Dimension, Body, Species,
In Mineral, Plant, Animal degrees?
  The 'Truth' is single, but His modes beget
All these imaginary entities.

Flash XIX.

When one says that the multiplicity of things is comprehended in the Unity of the One Real Being, this does not mean that they are the parts contained in an aggregate, or as objects contained in a receptacle; but that they are as the qualities inherent in the object qualified or as consequences flowing from their cause. Take, for instance, the half, the third, the fourth, and other fractions up to infinity, which are potentially[1] contained in the integer, one, though not actually manifested until they are exposed to view by repeating the various numbers and fractions.

It follows from this that when one says that the 'Truth' most glorious comprehends all beings, the meaning is that He comprehends them as a cause comprehends its consequences, not that He is a whole containing them as His parts, or as a vase containing things within it. God is too exalted above everything which is unworthy to touch the threshold of His holiness.[2]

These modes[3] are in the essence of the 'Truth,'
Like qualities which qualify the 'Truth';
  But part and whole, container and contained,
Exist not where God is, Who is the 'Truth.'

Flash XX.

The manifestation or concealment of the modes and facets —in other words, the circumstance that the outward aspect of Being does or does not clothe Himself with them—causes no change in the 'substance' of such Being or in His essential

[1] Potentiality and actuality are two of Aristotle's forms of thought, *dunamis* and *energeia* (*qūwat* and *fi'l*).

[2] God pervades everything, but everything is not God. Thus the strict Monism of some previous statements is considerably toned down.

[3] *Shā'n.* The 'Modalists' used the term 'modes' to indicate differences of form appearing in the One Substance (Harnack 'On Dogma,' iii. 53), and thus to avoid ditheism.

attributes, but only a change in His connections and relations, which, in fact, necessitates no change in His essence. For instance, if 'Amr gets up from the right of Zaid and goes and sits down on his left, the relation of Zaid to 'Amr in respect to position will be changed, but his essence and his inherent qualities will remain unchanged.

Thus, the One Real Being underlying all outward existence does not become more perfect by clothing Himself with noble forms, nor does He degrade Himself by manifestation in inferior theatres. Although the light of the sun illuminates at once the clean and the unclean, yet it undergoes no modifications in the purity of its light; it acquires neither the scent of musk nor the colour of the rose, the reproach of the thorn nor the disgrace of the rugged rock.

When the sun sheds his light for all to share,
It shines on foul things equally with fair;
Fair things do not augment its radiance,
Nor can foul things its purity impair.

Flash XXI.

The Absolute does not exist without the relative, and the relative is not formulated without the Absolute; but the relative stands in need of the Absolute, while the Absolute has no need of the relative. Consequently, the necessary connection of the two is mutual, but the need is on one side only, as in the case of the motion of a hand holding a key, and that of the key thus held.

O Thou whose sacred precincts none may see,
Unseen Thou makest all things seen to be;
Thou and we are not separate, yet still
Thou hast no need of us, but we of Thee.

Moreover, the Absolute requires a relative of some sort, not one particular relative, but any one that may be substituted for it. Now, seeing that there is no substitute for the Absolute, it is the Absolute alone who is the 'Qibla' of the needs of all relatives.

None by endeavour can behold Thy face,
Or access gain without prevenient grace ;[1]
For every man some substitute is found,
Thou hast no peer, and none can take Thy place.

Of accident or substance Thou hast naught,
Without constraint of cause Thy grace is wrought ;
Thou canst replace what's lost, but if Thou'rt lost,
In vain a substitute for Thee is sought.

It is in regard to His essence that the Absolute has no need of the relative. In other respects the manifestation of the names of His Divinity and the realization of the relations of His Sovereignty are clearly impossible otherwise than by means of the relative.

In me Thy beauty love and longing wrought :
Did I not seek Thee how could'st Thou be sought ?
My love is as a mirror in the which
Thy beauty into evidence is brought.

Nay, what is more, it is the 'Truth' who is Himself at once the lover and the beloved, the seeker and the sought. He is loved and sought in His character of the 'One who is all';[2] and He is lover and seeker when viewed as the sum of all particulars and plurality.[3]

O Lord, none but Thyself can fathom Thee,
Yet every mosque and church doth harbour Thee ;
I know the seekers and what 'tis they seek—
Seekers and sought are all comprised in Thee.

Flash XXII.

The substance of each individual thing may be described either as the epiphany of Very Being[4] in the 'intelligible world,' according to the particular facet whereof such thing is the monstrance, or as Very Being Himself made manifest *immediately*,[5] in the same intelligible world and according to the same facets. Consequently, each existing thing is either

[1] *Faiẓ i azal.*
[2] *Maqām i Jam' i Aḥadīyat.* Note the change of phrase.
[3] *Martaba i tafṣīl wa kithrat.*
[4] *Ta'ayyun i wajūd.*
[5] *Wajūd i muta'ayyīn.*

an epiphany of Very Being with the colour imparted to its exterior by the particular properties of its substance, or the Very Being Himself immediately made manifest with the same colouring.

The real substance of everything always abides, though concealed in the inner depth of the Very Being, while its sensible properties are manifest to outward sense. For it is impossible that the Divine 'Ideas'[1] in the intelligible world should be susceptible of evanescence, so that would involve atheism. [God is too exalted for such evanescence to be ascribed to His 'Ideas.'][2]

We are the facets and the modes of Being
Evolved from Mind[3]—yea, accidents of Being;
We're hidden in the cloak of non-existence,
But yet reflected in the glass of Being.[4]

[5][Consequently, everything is in reality and in fact either Being made manifest or an accident of Being thus manifested. The manifested accident is a quality of the manifested Being, and though in idea the quality is different from the thing qualified, yet in fact it is identical with it. Notwithstanding the difference in idea, the identity in fact justifies the attribution.[6]

In neighbour, friend, companion, Him we see,
In beggar's rags or robes of royalty;
In Union's cell or in Distraction's haunts,[7]
There's none but He—by God, there's none but He.[8]]

Flash XXIII.

Although the Very Being underlying all existence communicates Himself to all beings, both those in the intelligible and those in the sensible world, yet He does so in different

[1] *Ṣuwar i 'ilmīya.*
[2] Blank left as usual for the Arabic sentence.
[3] *I.e.*, the *'Ālam i 'ilm*, the intelligible world of the Divine 'Ideas.'
[4] Plotinus and the 'Gulshan i Rāz' make not-being the mirror of Very Being. Jāmī here inverts the metaphor.
[5] The following passage omitted in this text. It is probably a gloss which has crept into some manuscripts.
[6] *Ḥaml*, affirming a predicate of a subject.
[7] See Flash II.
[8] So 'Gulshan i Rāz,' l. 883: 'See but One, say but One, know but One.'

degrees [some superior to others]. And in each of these degrees He has certain names, attributes, and modes, applicable to that particular degree and not to the others; *e.g.*, the names Divinity and Sovereignty [are not applicable] to the degrees called Subordination and the Creature-state. Consequently, to apply the names 'Allah' and 'the Merciful,' etc., to created beings is sheer infidelity and heresy. And, similarly, to apply the names suitable to grades of created things to the Deity is the height of misconception and delusion.

> O you who deem yourself infallible,
> In certitude a very oracle,[1]
> Each grade of beings has its proper name:
> Mark this, or you'll become an infidel.[2]

Flash XXIV.

The Real Being is One alone, at once the true Existence and the Absolute. But He[3] possesses different degrees:

In the first degree He is unmanifested and unconditioned, and exempt from all limitation or relation. In this aspect He cannot be described by epithets or attributes, and is too holy to be designated by spoken or written words; neither does tradition furnish an expression for His Majesty, nor has reason the power to demonstrate the depth of His perfection. The greatest philosophers are baffled by the impossibility of attaining to knowledge of Him; His first characteristic is the lack of all characteristics, and the last result of the attempt to know Him is stupefaction.[4]

> To you convictions and presumptions wrought
> By evidence intuitive are naught;
> How can one prove your own reality
> To such as you who count all proofs as naught?

> However great our heavenly knowledge be,
> It cannot penetrate Thy sanctuary;
> Saints blest with visions and with light divine
> Reach no conceptions adequate to Thee.

[1] *Ṣiddīq*, veracious, like Abu Bakr 'aṣ-Ṣiddīq.'

[2] *Zindīq*.

[3] See note 2, p. 27.

[4] *Ḥairānī*. In the 'Manṭiq uṭ-Ṭair,' *Ḥairat* is the last valley in the Ṣūfī pilgrim's progress. To know God he must rise to ecstasy.

Our love,[1] the special grace of souls devout,
To reason seems a thing past finding out;
Oh, may it bring the dawn of certitude,
And put to flight the darksome hours of doubt!

The second degree is the self-display of Very Being in an epiphany containing in itself all the active, necessary and divine manifestations, as well as all the passive, contingent and mundane manifestations. This degree is named the 'First Emanation,'[2] because it is the first of all the manifestations of the Very Being; and above it there is no other degree than that of the 'Unmanifested.'

The third degree is named the 'Unity of the Whole Aggregate,'[3] which contains in itself all the active and efficient manifestations. It is named the degree of 'Divinity.'[4]

The fourth degree is the manifestation in detail of the degree named Divinity; it is the degree of the names and the theatres wherein they are manifested. These two last-named degrees refer to the outward aspect of Being wherein 'necessity'[5] is a universal condition.

The fifth degree is the 'Unity of the Whole Aggregate,' which includes all the passive manifestations whose characteristic is the potentiality of receiving impressions, *i.e.*, passivity. It is the degree of mundane existence and contingency.[6]

The sixth degree is the manifestation in detail of the preceding degree; it is the degree of the sensible world.[7] These two last degrees refer to the exterior of the intelligible world,[8] wherein contingence is one of the invariable qualities.

[1] Rūmī describes love as spiritual clairvoyance. See 'Masnavī, Introduction, p. xxviii.

[2] *Ta'ayyun i awwal*, usually called *'aql i kull*, universal reason—*i.e.*, *nous* or *Logos*, as by Jāmī himself in 'Salāman wa Absal.' 'The first thing created was reason' (Ḥadith).

[3] *Aḥadīyat i Jam'*, usually called *nafs i kull*, universal soul, *pneuma*.

[4] *Ilāhīyat*. See De Sacy's note in 'Notices et Extraits des Manuscrits,' x. 77.

[5] *Wajūb*. It belongs to the sphere of 'Necessary Being.'

[6] *Martaba i kaunīya i imkānīya*.

[7] *'Ālam*.

[8] The object of this distinction is to keep God from contact with matter. Contingency is not found in the *immediate* reflections of Being, but only in the reflections from the intelligible world of Divine Ideas.

It consists of the revelation of the Divine Mind to Himself under the forms of the substances of the contingent.

Consequently, in reality there is but One Sole Being, who is interfused in all these degrees and hierarchies which are only the details of the Unity ('Singleness').[1] 'Very Being' in these degrees is identical with them, just as these degrees when they were in the Very Being were identical therewith. ['God was, and there was not anything with Him.'][2]

The 'Truth' appears in all; would'st thou divine
How with Himself He doth all things combine?
  See the wine-froth: the wine in froth is froth,
Yet the froth on the wine is very wine.

'Tis the bright radiance of Eternity
That lights Not-being, as we men may see;
  Deem not the world is severed from the 'Truth':
In the world He's the world, in Him 'tis He.

Flash XXV.

The 'Truth of truths' which is the essential, most exalted Divine Being is the Reality in all things. He is One in Himself, and 'unique' in such wise that plurality cannot enter into Him; but by His multiple revelations and numerous phenomenal displays He is sometimes presented under the form of substantial independent entities,[3] and at other times under the form of accidental and dependent entities.[4] Consequently, the One Essential Being appears as multiple by reason of the numerous qualities of these substances and accidents, although in point of fact He is 'One,' and is in no wise susceptible of numbers or plurality.

Rase the words 'this' and 'that'; duality
Denotes estrangement and repugnancy;
  In all this fair and faultless universe
Naught but one Substance and one Essence see.[5]

[1] *Wāḥidīyat.* See note 2, p. 30.
[2] A saying attributed to Muhammad. A blank is left for it in this manuscript.
[3] *Ḥaqāiq i Jauharīya i maṭbū'a.*
[4] *Ḥaqāiq i 'araẓīya i ṭābi'a.*
[5] See note 8, p. 38.

This unique Substance, viewed as absolute and void of all phenomena, all limitations and all multiplicity, is the 'Truth.' On the other hand, viewed in His aspect of multiplicity and plurality, under which He displays Himself when clothed with phenomena, He is the whole created universe. Therefore the universe is the outward visible expression of the 'Truth,' and the 'Truth' is the inner unseen reality of the universe. The universe before it was evolved to outward view was identical with the 'Truth'; and the 'Truth' after this evolution is identical with the universe. Nay, more, in reality there is but One Real Being; His concealment [in the Divine Mind] and His manifestation [in the sensible world], His priority and His posteriority [in point of time], are all merely His relations and His aspects. 'It is He who is the first and the last, the exterior and the interior.'[1]

In the fair idols, goal of ardent youth,
And in all cynosures[2] lies hid the 'Truth';
  What, seen as relative, appears the world,
Viewed in its essence is the very 'Truth.'

When in His partial modes Truth shone out plain,
Straightway appeared this world of loss and gain;
  Were it and all who dwell there gathered back
Into the Whole, the 'Truth' would still remain.[3]

Flash XXVI.

The Shaikh[4] (may God be well pleased with him) says in the *Faṣṣ i Shu'aibī*, that the universe consists of accidents all pertaining to a single substance, which is the Reality underlying all existences. This universe is changed and renewed unceasingly at every moment and at every breath. Every instant one universe is annihilated and another resembling it takes its place, though the majority of men do not perceive this, as God most glorious has said: [' But they are in doubt regarding the new creation.'[5]]

[1] Koran, lvii. 3. *Cp.* Rev. i. 8, 'I am Alpha and Omega.'
[2] Literally, 'horizons'—*i.e.*, objects of aspiration.
[3] *I.e.*, the grade of plurality in Unity, or Universal Soul.
[4] Muḥiyi-ud-dīn Muḥammad Andalūsī, commonly called Ibn 'Arabi, died 638 A.H. Wrote the *Faṣūṣ-ul Ḥikam* (Haji Khalfa, iv. 424). Each section is named after some patriarch—*e.g.*, Shu'aib (Jethro).
[5] Koran, l. 14. See 'Gulshan i Rāz,' l. 670. Text omitted in this manuscript.

Among Rationalists,[1] no one has perceived this truth with the exception of the Asharians,[2] who recognise it in certain departments of the universe, to wit, 'accidents,' as when they say that accidents exist not for two moments together; and also with the exception of the Idealists,[3] called also Sophists, who recognise it in all parts of the universe, whether substances or accidents. But both these sects are in error in one part of their theory. The Asharians are wrong in asserting the existence of numerous substances—other than the One Real Being underlying all existence—on which substances, they say, depend the accidents which continually change and are renewed. They have not grasped the fact that the universe, together with all its parts, is nothing but a number of accidents, ever changing and being renewed at every breath, and linked together in a single substance, and at each instant disappearing and being replaced by a similar set. In consequence of this rapid succession, the spectator is deceived into the belief that the universe is a permanent existence. The Asharians themselves declare this when expounding the succession of accidents in their substances as involving continuous substitution of accidents, in such wise that the substances are never left wholly void of accidents similar to those which have preceded them. In consequence of this the spectator is misled into thinking that the universe is something constant and unique.[4]

The ocean does not shrink or vaster grow,
Though the waves ever ebb and ever flow;
The being of the world's a wave, it lasts
One moment, and the next it has to go.

In the world, men of insight may discern
A stream whose currents swirl and surge and churn,
And from the force that works within the stream
The hidden working of the 'Truth' may learn.

[1] *Ahl-i naẓr*, as opposed to *ahl-i shahūd*, men of spiritual intuition.
[2] The followers of Abū-l Ḥasan al Ashārī, died about 330 A.H. (Ibn Khallikan. ii. 227).
[3] The *Hasbāniya*.
[4] This is the Heracleitean doctrine that all phenomena are in constant flux, issuing from the 'Fiery Breath' (*Pneuma*) and remerged in it every moment. Jalāl-ud-dīn quotes the saying of 'Arqlitus' that 'Contraries are congruous,' the first suggestion of the Hegelian doctrine that contraries always involve a higher unity which embraces both. See Lumsden, 'Persian Grammar,' ii: 323.

As regards the Sophists, though they are right in asserting the ideality of the whole universe, they are wrong in failing to recognise the Real Being underlying it, who clothes Himself with the forms and accidents of the sensible universe, and appears to us under the guise of phenomena and multiplicity; likewise in denying any manifestation of Real Being in the grades of visible things under the guise of these forms and accidents, whereas in truth these accidents and forms are only manifested to outward view by the operation of that underlying Real Being.

Philosophers devoid of reason find
This world a mere idea of the mind;
'Tis an idea—but they fail to see
The great Idealist who looms behind.

But the men gifted with spiritual intuition see that the Majesty of the 'Truth,' most glorious and most exalted, reveals Himself at every breath in a fresh revelation,[1] and that He never repeats the same revelation; that is to say, He never reveals Himself during two consecutive moments under the guise of the same phenomena and modes, but every moment presents fresh phenomena and modes.

The forms which clothe existence only stay
One moment, in the next they pass away;
This subtle point is proven by the text,
'Its fashion altereth from day to day.'[2]

The root of this mystery lies in the fact that the Majesty of the 'Truth' most glorious possesses 'names' opposed[3] to one another, some being beautiful and some terrible; and these names are all in continuous operation,[4] and no cessation of such operation is possible for any of them. Thus, when one of the contingent substances, through the concurrence of

[1] See 'Masnavī,' p. 24.
[2] Koran lv. 29.
[3] *Lutf* and *Qahr*, or *Jamāl* and *Jalāl*, the opposite Divine attributes of mercy and vengeance, beauty and terror. The Divine economy is sometimes represented as effected by the eternal struggle between these two opposite phases of Deity, as manifested in Adam and Iblīs, Abraham and Nimrod, Moses and Pharaoh, etc. (see 'Masnavī, p. 301), a daring Monist hypothesis, which, needless to say, is not pursued into its consequences.
[4] These 'names,' like the Stoic *logoi*, are sometimes spoken of as ideas, sometimes as forces or energies.

the requisite conditions, and the absence of opposing conditions, becomes capable of receiving the Very Being, the mercy of the Merciful takes possession of it, and the Very Being is infused[1] into it; and the Very Being thus externalized,[2] through being clothed with the effects and properties of such substances, presents Himself under the form of a particular phenomenon, and reveals Himself under the guise of this phenomenon. Afterwards, by the operation of the terrible Omnipotence which requires the annihilation of all phenomena and all semblance of multiplicity, this same substance is stripped of these phenomena. At the very moment that it is thus stripped this same substance is reclothed with another particular phenomenon, resembling the preceding one, through the operation of the mercy of the Merciful One. The next moment this latter phenomenon is annihilated by operation of the terrible Omnipotence, and another phenomenon is formed by the mercy of the Merciful One; and so on for as long as God wills. Thus, it never happens that the Very Being is revealed for two successive moments under the guise of the same phenomenon. At every moment one universe is annihilated and another similar to it takes its place. But he who is blinded by these veils, to wit, the constant succession of similar phenomena and like conditions, believes that the universe constantly endures in one and the same state, and never varies from time to time.

The glorious God, whose bounty, mercy, grace,
And loving-kindness all the world embrace,
  At every moment brings a world to naught,
And fashions such another in its place.

All gifts soever unto God are due,
Yet special gifts from special 'names' ensue;
  At every breath one 'name' annihilates,
And one creates all outward things anew.

The proof that the universe is nothing more than a combination of accidents united in a single essence, *i.e.*, the

[1] *Ifāẓat*, production by emanation. See 'Notices et Extraits des Manscrits,' x., p. 66.
[2] *Sein* evolved into *dasein*.

'Truth' or Very Being, lies in the fact that when one comes to define the nature of existing things these definitions include nothing beyond 'accidents.' For example, when one defines man as a 'rational animal'; and animal as a 'growing and sentient body, possessed of the faculty of voluntary movement'; and body as a 'substance possessing three dimensions'; and substance as an 'entity which exists *per se* and is not inherent in any other subject'; and entity as 'an essence possessed of reality and necessary being'—all the terms used in these definitions come under the category of 'accidents,' except this vague essence which is discerned behind these terms. For 'rational' signifies an essence endued with reason; 'that which is growing' signifies an essence endued with the faculty of growth; and so on. This vague essence is, in fact, the 'Truth,' the Very Being, who is self-existent, and who causes all these accidents to exist. And when the philosophers allege that these terms do not express the differences themselves, but only the invariable marks of these differences whereby we express them, because it is impossible to express the true differences otherwise than by these invariable marks or others more recondite still, this assumption is inadmissible and undeserving of serious attention. And even if we admit it as a hypothesis, we affirm that whatever is essential in relation to special substances is accidental in relation to the Very Truth; for though this alleged essential quality is part of the essence of a particular substance, it is extraneous to the Very Truth upon whom it is dependent. And to say that there is any substantial entity other than the One Essential Being is the height of error, especially when the spiritual intuition of the men of truth, which is borrowed from the lamp of prophecy, attests the contrary,[1] and when their opponents cannot cite any proofs in favour of their own view. ['God saith what is true, and directeth man in the right path.'[2]]

[1] *Cp.* 1 Cor. ii. 15, 'He that is spiritual judgeth all things, yet he himself is judged of no man.' Or, as Hegelians would put it, the deliverances of intuitive reason are not to be tried by the canons of the discursive reason (*verstand*).

[2] Koran, xxxiii. 4. A blank is again left for the text in this manuscript.

Truth is not proved by terms and demonstrations,
Nor seen when hidden by concrete relations;[1]
  The 'Canon' is no 'Cure' for ignorance,
  Nor can 'Deliv'rance' come from 'Indications.'[2]

If at each 'Stage' thy course diverted be
To different 'Goals,' true goal thou'lt never see;
  And till the veil is lifted from thine eyes
The sun of Truth will never 'Rise' for thee.[3]

Strive to cast off the veil, not to augment
Book-lore: no books will further thy intent.
  The germ of love to God grows not in books;
Shut up thy books, turn to God and repent.

The completest mask and the densest veils of the beauty of the One Real Being are produced by the manifold limitations which are found in the outward aspect of Being and which result from His being clothed with the properties and effects of the archetypes indwelling in the Divine Knowledge,[4] which is the inner side of Being. To those blinded by these veils it seems that the archetypes exist in these outward sensible objects, whereas in point of fact these outward objects never attain a particle[5] of those real archetypes, but are and will always continue in their original not-being. What exists and is manifested is the 'Truth,' but this is only in regard to His being clothed with the properties and effects of the archetypes, and not in regard to His condition when bare of all these properties; for in this latter case inwardness and concealment are amongst His inherent qualities. Consequently, in reality the Very Being never ceases to abide in His Essential Unity, wherein He was from all eternity and wherein He will

[1] *Quyūd.*

[2] Alluding to four famous works of Ibn Sīnā (Avicena), 'Shifā,' 'Qānūn, 'Nijāt,' and 'Ishārāt.'

[3] Alluding to 'Mawāqif,' a theological work by Al Ijī; 'Maqāṣid,' by Al Taftāzānī; and 'Maṭāli',' a work on logic by Al Ormawī. See Otto Loth, 'Catalogue of India Office Arabic Manuscripts,' pp. 114, 460, and 143.

[4] *A'yān i thābitah dar ḥazrat i 'ilm*, the Ideas or archetypes in Plato's 'Intelligible World' (see 'Notices et Extraits des Manuscrits,' vol. x., p. 65 . *'Ain* has the double meaning of 'eye' and 'essence,' and its derivatives *A'yān* and *Ta'ayyun* are used to denote the reflections of the One Being; in other words, His emanations which constitute the existences or substances in the world of visible and sensible phenomena (*'Ālam i 'Ain*).

[5] Literally, 'smell.'

endure to all eternity. But to the vulgar, who are blinded by these veils, the Very Being seems to be relative and phenomenal, and wearing the form of the multiplicity of these properties and effects, and He seems manifold to such persons.

Being's a sea in constant billows rolled,[1]
'Tis but these billows that we men behold;
  Sped from within, they rest upon the sea,
And like a veil its actual form enfold.

Being's the essence of the Lord of all,
All things exist in Him and He in all;
  This is the meaning of the Gnostic phrase,
'All things are comprehended in the All.'

[2][When one thing is manifested in another, the thing manifested is different from the thing which is the theatre of the manifestation—*i.e.*, the thing manifested is one thing and its theatre another. Moreover, that which is manifested in the theatre is the image or form of the thing manifested, not its reality or essence. But the case of the Very Being, the Absolute, is an exception, all whose manifestations are identical with the theatres wherein they are manifested, and in all such theatres He is manifested in His own essence.

They say, How strange! This peerless beauty's face
Within the mirror's heart now holds a place;[3]
  The marvel's not the face, the marvel is
That it should be at once mirror and face.

All mirrors in the universe I ween
Display Thy image with its radiant sheen—
  Nay, in them all, so vast Thy effluent grace,
'Tis Thyself, not Thine image, that is seen.

The 'Truth,' the Very Being, along with all His modes, His attributes, connections, and relations, which constitute the real existence of all beings, is immament in the real existence

[1] See Masnavī, p. 42.
[2] The following passage in brackets is omitted in this manuscript.
[3] In the 'Gulshan i Rāz,' l. 134, Very Being is said to be reflected in the mirror of not-being.

of each being. Hence it has been said, 'The All exists in all things.' The author of the *Gulshan i Rāz* says:

> 'If you cleave the heart of one drop of water
> There will issue from it a hundred pure oceans.'[1]]

Every power and every act manifested as proceeding from the theatres of manifestation proceed in reality from the 'Truth' manifested in these theatres, and not from the theatres themselves. The Shaikh (may God be well pleased with him) says in the *Ḥikmat i 'Aliyya*:[2] 'Outward existence (*'ain*) can perform no act of itself; its acts are those of its Lord immanent in it; hence this outward existence is passive, and action cannot be attributed to it.' Consequently, power and action are ascribed to the creature (*'abd*) because of the manifestation of the 'Truth' under the form of the creature, and not because such action is really effected by the creature himself. [Read the text: 'God hath created thee, both thee and the works of thy hands'[3]], and recognise the fact that thy existence, thy power, and thine actions come from the Majesty of Him who has no equal.[4]

> Both power and being are denied to us,
> The lack of both is what's ordained for us;
> But since 'tis He who lives within our forms,
> Both power and action are ascribed to us.
>
> Your 'self' is non-existent, knowing one!
> Deem not your actions by yourself are done;
> Make no wry faces at this wholesome truth—
> 'Build the wall ere the fresco is begun.'
>
> Why vaunt thy 'self' before those jealous eyes?[5]
> Why seek to deal in this false merchandise?
> Why feign to be existent of thyself?
> Down with these vain conceits and foolish lies!

[1] Verse 146.

[2] The Shaikh Muḥiyi-ud-dīn Ibn al'Arabī. The 'Ḥikmat i 'Aliyya' is the first section of his 'Faṣūṣ-ul Ḥikam.

[3] Koran, xxxvii. 94. A blank left for the text.

[4] The Ṣūfīs call God, the 'One Real Agent'—*Fā'il-i Ḥaqīqī.* Deter minism is a necessary corollary of Monism.

[5] *Cp.* the Ḥadith, 'God is more jealous than Sa'd' ('Masnavī,' p. 29, note). Self-assertion is presumption towards God.

Flash XXVII.

Since the qualities, states, and actions manifested in the theatres are in reality to be ascribed to the Very Being manifested in those theatres, it follows that if a certain evil or imperfection is found in any of them, it may possibly be caused by the non-existence of something else; for Being, *quâ* Being, is pure good; and whenever it seems to us that something existent contains evil, *that* is owing to the lack of something else which ought to exist, and not to the really existing Being, *quâ* Being.[1]

All good and all perfection that you see
Are of the 'Truth,' which from all stain is free;
Evil and pain result from some defect,
Some lack of normal receptivity.

Philosophers have alleged that the proposition 'Very Being is pure good' is a necessary (self-evident) one.[2] By way of illustration, they have given some examples. Thus, they say cold, which spoils the fruit and is an evil in relation to the fruit, is not an evil [absolutely], because it is one of the qualities [of Being], and in this respect one of His perfections; but [it is evil] because it prevents the fruit attaining the perfection proper to it. Thus too killing, which is an evil, is not an evil by reason of the murderer's power of killing, nor by reason of the power of the instrument to cut, nor of the liability of the body of the person killed to be cut; but [it is an evil] because it deprives a person of life, which is the mere negation [of something positive];[3] and so on.

[1] 'Being is good in whatever it be. If a thing contains evil, *that* proceeds from "other"' ('Gulshan i Rāz,' l. 871). This represents evil as something positive. So Dante says matter is intractable ('Paradiso,' Canto I.). Augustine, like Jāmī, makes evil merely a deficiency of good. See 'Confessions,' Book VII., chapter xii.

[2] *Ẓarūrat.* Necessary truths are those of which the contrary is inconceivable. Of course, in Jāmī's time necessity of thought was supposed to involve necessity of the object of thought.

[3] The ideas that God is all and determines all, and that evil is unreal, may seem true to men like Augustine, glowing with religious emotion, but are untenable in practice, and if translated into hard theological formulas become a stumbling-block. Jalāl-ud-dīn quietly drops them when it comes to a question of practice.

Wherever Being's ambit doth extend,
Good and nought else but good is found, O friend;
All evil comes from 'not-being,' to wit,
From 'other,' and on 'other' must depend.[1]

Flash XXVIII.

Shaikh Ṣadr-ud-dīn Qūniavī[2] (may God sanctify his secret) says in the book *Nuṣūṣ*: 'Knowledge is one of the qualities pertaining to Being; that is to say, that every existing substance is endued with knowledge; and the difference in the degrees of knowledge results from the differences of these substances in their reception, whether perfect or imperfect, of Being. Thus a substance capable of receiving Being in a most complete and perfect way is capable of receiving knowledge in the same way; and that which is only capable of receiving Being imperfectly is endued with knowledge in the same degree. This difference originates in the stronger or weaker influence of 'necessity'[3] or 'contingency' over each substance. In every substance in which the influence of 'necessity' is the stronger, Being and knowledge are most perfect; in the remainder, in which the influence of 'contingency' is more prevalent, Being and knowledge are more imperfect.'

It would seem that what the Shaikh states as to knowledge specially being a quality appertaining to Being is meant to convey one example only, because all the other perfections which are likewise qualities pertaining to Being, such as life, power, will, etc., are in the same position as knowledge.

Certain other [Ṣūfīs] have said: 'No single existent thing is without the quality of knowledge'; but knowledge is of two kinds, one ordinarily called knowledge and the other not so called. Both kinds, according to the men of truth, belong to the category of knowledge, because they recognise the

[1] 'Gulshan i Rāz,' l. 871.

[2] 'An-Nuṣūṣ fī taḥqīq i ṭaur il makhṣūṣ,' by the celebrated Ṣūfī Shaikh Ṣadr-ud-dīn Muḥammad bin Isḥāq al Qūniavī, died 672 A.H. See Haji Khalfa, vi. 349.

[3] The more 'necessary being' a thing has, the less it has of 'contingent being'—*i.e.*, less intermixture with not-being. See note 2, p. 33.

immanence of the essential knowledge of the 'Truth' most glorious and most exalted in all things whatsoever. It is in the second class that we must place "water," for example, which is not ordinarily considered as possessed of knowledge. But we see that it distinguishes between up and down hill; it avoids the rise and runs downwards; again, it sinks into porous bodies, whilst it only wets the surface of dense bodies and passes over them, etc. Therefore, it is by virtue of the quality of knowledge that it runs, according to the capacity of one object to admit it, and the absence of opposing properties in such objects. But, in this degree, knowledge is manifested only under the form of nature.[1] In this manner knowledge is immanent in all other existing things; or, rather, all perfections pertaining to Being are immanent in all things without exception.

Being, with all its latent qualities,
Doth permeate all mundane entities,
  Which, when they can receive them, show them forth
In the degrees of their capacities.

Flash XXIX.

Just as the 'Truth,' the Very Being, in virtue of His absolute purity, is immanent in the substances of all beings in such wise as to be essentially identical with these substances, as these substances are, when in Him, identical with Him; in like manner His perfect qualities are entirely and absolutely immanent in all qualities of the substances in such wise as to be identical with their qualities, even as their qualities when in those perfect qualities were identical therewith. For example, the quality of knowledge, in the knowledge of the knower of particulars,[2] is identical with this knowledge of particulars, and in the knowledge of him who knows universals[2] is identical with this knowledge of universals; in active and passive[3] knowledge it is identical

[1] *I.e.*, in unconscious objects. Thus Aristotle says plants seek their own perfection unconsciously, while man does it consciously.

[2] *Juzviyāt* and *kulliyāt.*

[3] *Fi'lī* and *infi'ālī*—*i.e.*, knowledge gained by inference and reasoning, and that conveyed by immediate consciousness and sensation.

with such knowledge; in ecstatic and mystic[1] knowledge it is identical with that kind of knowledge—similarly down to the knowledge of those beings not ordinarily classed as having knowledge, wherein it is identical with such knowledge in a manner suitable to the character of such beings, and so on for the other divine attributes and qualities.[2]

Thy essence permeates all entities,
As do Thy attributes all qualities;
In Thee they're absolute, but when displayed,
They're only seen in relative degrees.[3]

[[4]The reality of existence is the essence[5] of the 'Truth' most glorious and most exalted; the modes, relations, and aspects of existence are His attributes;[6] His manner of manifesting Himself in the vesture of these relations and aspects is His action and His impress;[7] the phenomena manifested and proceeding from this self-revelation are the products of His impress.[8]

Th' essential modes in earth and heavens present[9]
Facets of Him who's veiled and immanent;
Hence, O inquirer, learn what essence is,
What attribute, what cause, what consequent.]

Flash XXX

In some passages of the *Faṣūṣ* the Shaikh[10] (may God show mercy upon him) seems to point to the view that the existence of all contingent substances and of all perfections dependent on that existence [[11] is to be ascribed to the Majesty of the 'Truth' most glorious and most exalted;

[1] *Wijdānī* and *dhauqī*.
[2] Here the last quatrain in Flash XXVIII. is repeated.
[3] *Taqayyud*, limitation.
[4] The following passage in brackets is omitted in this manuscript.
[5] *Dhāt*.
[6] *Ṣifāt*.
[7] *Fi'il* and *ta'thīr*.
[8] *Athār*.
[9] *Dunyā wa dīn*, earth and the celestial spheres, the 'theatres' or monstrances of the Divine perfections, rather than the world and the Moslem Church (the ordinary meaning).
[10] See note 4, p. 42.
[11] This passage in square brackets is found in one British Museum manuscript. It certainly makes the sense clearer.

whilst in other passages he seems to say that what is ascribed to the Majesty of the 'Truth' is merely an emanation[1] of Being; and as regards the qualities dependent on existence, they are effects produced by the substances themselves. These two statements may be thus reconciled: The Majesty of the 'Truth' most glorious is revealed in two manners—the first the inward, subjective[2] revelation, which the Ṣūfīs name 'Most Holy Emanation';[3] it consists in the self-manifestation of the 'Truth' to His own consciousness from all eternity under the forms of substances,[4] their characteristics and capacities. The second revelation is the outward objective manifestation, which is called 'Holy Emanation';[5] it consists in the manifestation of the 'Truth,' with the impress of the properties and marks of the same substances.[6] This second revelation ranks after the first; it is the theatre wherein are manifested to sight the perfections which in the first revelation were contained potentially in the characteristics and capacities of the substances.

One grace a host of suppliant forms designed,
A second to each one his lot assigned;
The first had no beginning—of the last,
Which springs from it, no end can be divined.[7]

Wherefore, the ascription of existence and the perfections dependent thereon] to the 'Truth' most glorious and most exalted has regard to the two revelations taken together; and the ascription to the 'Truth' of existence alone, and of its dependents to the substances, has reference to the second revelation; for the only result of the second revelation is the emanation of Being into the substances, and so making

[1] *Ifāẓat*, production by emanation. See De Sacy's article on 'Jorjānī's Definitions' (Notices et Extraits des Manuscrits,' x., p. 66).
[2] *'Ilmī.*
[3] *Faiẓ i Aqdas* (see 'Notices et Extraits,' x., p. 66), the first emanation, or *'aql i kull.*
[4] *I.e.*, the 'archetypal ideas' of the intelligible world, *'ālam i 'ilmī.*
[5] *Faiẓ i Muqaddas*, the second emanation, or *nafs i kull* (Anima mundi).
[6] *I.e.*, *'ālam i 'ainī*, the sensible world, the copy of the intelligible world.
[7] The sensible world issues from the intelligible world, and will continue 'as long as God wills.'

visible what had already been included in them by the first revelation.

Mark well this subtle point—each quality,
Each action that in substances we see,
  On one side is attributed to us,
On one to 'TRUTH,' the sole Reality.

APPENDIX.[1]

Whereas my aim and object in giving these explanations and hints has been to call attention to the essential omnipresence of the Majesty of the 'Truth' most glorious, and to the immanence of His light in all the grades [of sensible existence], to the end that the pilgrims and aspirants endued with knowledge and reflection may not neglect the contemplation of His Being while preoccupied with any other being, and that they may not forget the consideration of the perfection of His attributes while paying regard solely to the qualities manifested [in the sensible universe], and whereas what has been said above is sufficient for this purpose, and satisfactorily accomplishes this end, I therefore conclude the book at this point, merely adding the following quatrains:

Jāmī! leave polishing of phrases, cease
Writing and chanting fables, hold thy peace;
  Dream not that 'Truth' can be revealed by words:
From this fond dream, O dreamer, find release![2]

Beggars in tattered clothes their rents should hide,
And lovers take discretion for their guide,
  And, since words do but veil the Loved One's face,
'Tis well for us in silence to abide.

How long wilt thou keep clanging like a bell?
Be still, and learn this flood of words to quell;
  Thou'lt never come to hold the pearl of 'Truth'
Till thou art made all ear, as is the shell.[3]

[1] *Tadhyīl* in one manuscript; another has 'Flash.'

[2] The 'Masnavī' finishes in the same strain. See the parable of the Moslem who, by childlike faith, prevailed over his learned fellow-travellers (p. 304).

[3] *I.e.*, the oyster-shell (see 'Gulshan i Rāz,' l. 572). Here in one manuscript there follow two quatrains which are mere variations of the same theme.

Thou who for grief hast soiled thy weeds with dust,[1]
Soil not thy lips with speech (for soil it must);
While thou can'st commune silently with Him,
Rather than speak stop up thy mouth with dust!

This treatise was completed by the help of God and the favour of His grace. May He bless Muḥammad and his family and his companions!

[1] Read *Khākat ba kafan.* V. L., *Chākat—i.e.*, in token of mourning.

APPENDICES

APPENDIX I

GHAZZĀLĪ ON 'TAUḤĪD'[1]

PRAISE be to God, the Creator and Restorer of all things; who does whatsoever He pleases, who is Master of the glorious throne and mighty force, and directs His sincere servants into the right way and the straight path; who favoureth them who have once borne testimony to the Unity by preserving their confessions from the darkness of doubt and hesitation; who directs them to follow His chosen apostle, upon whom be the blessing and peace of God; and to go after his most honourable companions, to whom He hath vouchsafed His assistance and direction, which is revealed to them in His essence and operation by the excellencies of His attributes, to the knowledge whereof no man attains but he that hath been taught by hearing.[2] To these, as touching His essence, He maketh known that He is One, and hath no partner; singular, without anything like Him; uniform, having no contrary; separate, having no equal.[3] He is ancient, having no first; eternal, having no beginning; remaining for ever, having no end; continuing to eternity without any termination. He persists, never ceasing to be; remains without falling; and never did cease, nor ever shall cease, to be described by glorious attributes; nor is subject to any decree so as to be determined by any precise limits or set times, but is the First and the Last, and is within and without.

[1] This passage is given in Pococke's 'Specimen Historiæ Arabum' (Oxoniæ, 1650), p. 284, and this translation of it by Ockley is copied from Hughes's 'Notes on Muḥammadanism.'

[2] 'Faith cometh by hearing' (Rom. x. 17).

[3] This is directed against the Christian Trinity, which all Moslems suppose to be the equivalent of Tritheism.

What God is not.—He, glorified be His name, is not a body endued with form,[1] nor a substance circumscribed with limits or determined by measure; neither does He resemble bodies, as they are capable of being measured and divided. Neither is He a substance, nor do substances exist in Him; nor is He an accident, nor do accidents exist in Him. Neither is He like to anything that exists, nor is anything like to Him; nor is He determinate in quantity, nor comprehended by bounds, nor circumscribed by differences of situation, nor contained in the heavens. He sits upon the throne, after that manner which He Himself hath described, and in that sense which He Himself means, which is a sitting far removed from any notion of contact, or resting upon, or local situation; but both the throne itself, and whatsoever is upon it, are sustained by the goodness of His power, and are subject to the grasp of His hand.[2] But He is above the throne and above all things, even to the utmost ends of the earth; but so above as at the same time not to be a whit nearer the throne and the heaven; since He is exalted by (infinite) degrees above the throne, no less than He is exalted above the earth, and at the same time He is near to everything that hath being—nay, 'nearer to men than their jugular veins, and is witness to everything'[3]—though His nearness is not like the nearness of bodies, as neither is His essence like the essence of bodies. Neither doth He exist in anything,[4] neither doth anything exist in Him; but He is too high to be contained in any place, and too holy to be determined by time; for He was before time and place were created, and is now after the same manner as He always was. He is also distinct from the creatures in His attributes, neither is there anything besides Himself in His essence, nor is His essence in any other be-

[1] This is directed against the Anthropomorphists, the Kerāmians, and the Moshabbehites. See Sale, 'Preliminary Discourse to Koran,' Section viii.

[2] Just like Philo, Ghazzālī struggles with the anthropomorphic language of the Koran, in order to remove God from contact with matter, which his reading of Greek philosophy had taught him was evil.

[3] 'Surah,' l. 15.

[4] Directed againsi those who held the doctrine of Incarnation, the Ḥalūlians.

sides Him. He is too holy to be subject to change or any local motion; neither do any accidents dwell in Him, nor any contingencies before Him; but He abides through all generations with His glorious attributes, free from all danger of dissolution. As to the attribute of perfection, He wants no addition. As to being, He is known to exist by the apprehension of the understanding; and He is seen as He is by immediate intuition, which will be vouchsafed out of His mercy and grace to the holy in the eternal mansion, completing their joy by the vision of His glorious presence.[1]

His Power.— . . . His is the dominion and the excellency and the creation and the command.[2] . . . His excellency consists in His creating and producing, and His unity in communicating existence and the beginning of being.[3] . . .

His Knowledge.—He knows what is secret and conceals it, and views the conceptions of minds and the motions of thoughts, and the inmost recesses of secrets, by a knowledge ancient and eternal, that never ceased to be His attribute from eternal eternity, and not by any new knowledge superadded to His essence. . . .

His Will.—He doth will those things to be that are, and disposes of all accidents. Nothing passes in the empire or the kingdom, neither small nor great, nor good nor evil, nor profitable nor hurtful, nor faith nor infidelity, nor knowledge nor ignorance, nor prosperity nor adversity, nor increase nor decrease, nor obedience nor rebellion, but by His determinate counsel and decree and His definite sentence and will. . . . He it is who gave all things their beginning; He is the Creator and Restorer, the sole Operator of what He pleases; there is no reversing His decree nor delaying what He hath determined; nor is there any refuge to man from his rebellion against Him, but only His help and mercy; nor hath any man any power to perform any duty towards Him but through His love and will.[4] . . .

[1] The beatific vision of Dante's Paradise. The idea came in the last resort from the Platonists, from whom Ghazzālī also probably got it.

[2] 'Surah,' vii. 52, 'Are not creation and command of Him?'

[3] All created existence is one, and proceeds from the One.

[4] This language shows how easily the conception of Monotheism passed into Monism—*i.e.*, the religious view into the philosophic.

His Word.—Furthermore, He doth command, forbid, promise and threaten, by an eternal ancient Word subsisting in His essence.[1] Neither is it like to the word of the creatures, nor doth it consist in a voice arising from the commotion of the air or the collision of bodies, nor letters which are separated by the joining together of the lips or the motion of the tongue. The Koran, the Law, the Gospel, and the Psalter, are books sent down by Him to His apostles, and the Koran, indeed, is read with tongues, written in books, and kept in hearts; yet as subsisting in the essence of God it doth not become liable to separation and division when it is transferred to hearts and to papers.[2] Thus, Moses also heard the word of God without voice or letter, even as the saints behold the essence of God without substance or accident. . . .

His Works.—He exists after such a manner that nothing besides Him hath any being but what is produced by His operation, and floweth from His justice after the best, most excellent, most perfect, and most just models.[3] . . .

All things were created by Him—genii, men, the devil, angels, heaven, earth, animals, plants, substance, accident, intelligible, sensible. He created them by His power out of mere privation, and brought them into light when as yet they were nothing at all,[4] but He Himself alone existed from all eternity, neither was there any other with Him. Now, He created all things in the beginning for the manifestation of His power and His will and the confirmation of His word, which was true from all eternity. Not that He stood in need of them nor wanted them, but He manifestly declared His glory in creating and producing and commanding, without being under any obligation nor out of necessity. . . .

He rewards those that worship Him for their obedience on account of His promise and beneficence, not of their merit, nor of necessity, since there is nothing which He can be tied

[1] See Hirschfeld 'On the Qorān,' p. 14. The *Logos.*

[2] This is the opinion that the Koran was uncreated condemned by Al Mamūn in the second century A.H. See Hirschfeld on the 'I'jāz (miracle) of the Qorān,' p. 8.

[3] Here we have Plato's ideas or archetypes in the intelligible world, after the pattern of which sensible objects are formed.

[4] Privation, the Greek 'not-being.' Note also 'substance' and 'accident.'

to perform; nor can any injustice be supposed in Him; nor can He be under any obligation to any person whatsoever. That His creatures, however, should be bound to serve Him ariseth from His having declared by the tongues of the prophets that it was due to Him from them. The worship of Him is not simply the dictate of the understanding, but He sent messengers to carry to men His commands and promises and threats, whose veracity He proved by manifest miracles,[1] whereby men are obliged to give credit to them in those things that they relate.[2]

[1] Muḥammad's miracles were the *Āyāt*, signs (texts of the Koran). See Hirschfeld 'On the Qorān,' pp. 1, 8.

[2] Ghazzālī speaks as an orthodox Moslem, but Greek influences are manifest in this passage, and his statements on the thorny subject of grace and works recall those of the great Christian Platonist Augustine.

APPENDIX II

PLOTINUS

From Anaxagoras onwards the main principle of Greek philosophy was dualism, the opposition of the One and the many, God and the world. In an often-quoted passage Plato says the Ideal Good is beyond existence (*epekeina tēs ousias*).

Next in the descending scale he placed the 'Intelligible World' of Ideas or archetypes, conceived by reason (*Nous*). Then came the 'Sensible World' of phenomena, which were only copies of the divine archetypes reproduced in matter.[1] This matter was of itself non-existent (*mē on*) ; in fact, a mere potentiality of taking the imprints of the archetypes.

With the Stoics monism made its appearance, and took the place of the previous dualism. For Plato's 'Ideas' they substituted *Logoi*, thoughts, forms, or forces immanent in the universe. And these *Logoi* were often spoken of as all summed up in the one *Logos*. Most Stoics, like Epictetus and Marcus Aurelius, regarded the universe as *natura naturans*, manifested *Logos* or *Anima Mundi;* others regarded the *Logoi* as only functions of matter (*natura naturata*).

Philo, the Alexandrian Jew, who lived at the same time as St. Paul, managed to combine this *Logos* doctrine with the Hebrew Scriptures.[2] By allegorical interpretation he identified the Stoic *Logoi* with the angels mentioned in the Scriptures, and at the same time he reduced the personal Yahveh of the Scriptures to the abstract Being of Greek philosophy.

[1] See 'Masnavī,' p. 226.

[2] The Book of Wisdom, probably the work of a Hellenizing Jew, prepared the way for Philo, but the cautious writer speaks not of Greek 'Logos,' but of Hebrew 'Wisdom,' as the first effluent, the mirror and express image of the Deity (Wisd. vii. 26).

The Hebrew prophets had almost personified the 'Word of the Lord' and 'Wisdom'; and *Logos*, with its double meaning of thought and word (*ratio* and *oratio*), was easily identified with 'Word' and 'Wisdom.' As Dr. Hirschfeld has pointed out, *Amr* and *Kalima* underwent a similar process in the Koran.[1] The *Logos*, having been thus personified, plays a very important part in Philo's system. It becomes the Demiurge or Architect of the world. The metaphor of generation is employed to picture the mode of its operation. Sometimes it is figured as masculine, sometimes as a female agent, but in either case it is one of the parents of the world of phenomena.[2] On the whole it may be said that Philo's leading principles were, first, to remove the Deity far away from any contact with matter, and, secondly, to explain the existence of the world by the hypothesis of intermediate and subordinate agencies through whom the Deity worked, so as not to touch matter Himself.

Hence Philo's system was dualism. And this dualistic tendency was fostered by the growing influence of Manicheism. Manes, who formulated this old Persian dualism, did not live till the third century A.D., but many of the Gnostic sects of the second century A.D. held what were in fact Manichean opinions. And this led some, like Basileides, to emphasize the separation of the Deity from the evil material world. Basileides, for instance, though he firmly believed in God, declared in hyperbolical language that He was *ouk ōn*, 'without existence' in the sense of the phenomenal existence known to man.[3] Others, like Valentinus, imagined a series of Æons or intermediate Intelligences, so as to remove the transcendental God as far as possible from contact with matter. These Æons were possibly the prototypes of the Ṣūfī Ten Intelli-

[1] 'New Researches in the Qorān,' 1902, p. 15. Some Ṣūfī theologians identified Muḥammad with 'Universal Reason,' or Logos. See Palmer's 'Oriental Mysticism,' p. 43, and 'Masnavī,' p. 179.

[2] Yonge's translation of Philo, i. 359 and ii. 205 (quoted in Appendix to 'Masnavī'). Tholuck, when he encounters this idea in 'Masnavī,' p. 77, and 'Gulshan i Rāz,' l. 622, finds it shocking; but few like to face the historical antecedents or parallells of cherished tenets.

[3] See Mansel's 'Gnostic Heresies,' p. 147.

gences and of the Celestial Hierarchies of Dionysius, which supplied the frame of Dante's Paradise.

Plotinus, who lived in the third century A.D, was a mystic who busied himself with philosophy only to seek corroboration of his mystical beliefs. He started with the conviction that the One was all in all, and that all phenomena had no existence apart from it. He tried to reach a conception of the transcendental One by abstracting or stripping off all limitations and conditions incident to phenomenal existence, and by assuming that the residuum was the One. But as this residuum was void of all positive contents, it could not be conceived by common reason, and could be described only in negative terms, as 'Unconditioned,' 'Infinite,' 'Incomprehensible,' and the like. Reason could not say what it was, but only what it was not. His position thus seems to be precisely that of agnosticism, as expounded in H. Spencer's 'First Principles.' But here the resemblance ceases. Plotinus held that the impotence of reason to conceive the Absolute proved that ordinary reason must be entirely discarded in these matters, so as to give free play to the superior faculty of spiritual intuition or intuitive reason (*Nous*), which alone is competent to deal with them.[1] This faculty discerns the One to be no mere negation, but a supreme energy of self-manifestation.[2] Without any diminution or decrease of itself the One ever pours forth or rays out effluences. Hence arises an image or reflection of the One in *Nous* or Reason, the First Emanation, comprehending all being and all thought. From this proceeded in like manner the Second Emanation, called the 'World-soul,'[3] *Psychē*, which acted as the mediator between the supra-sensible and the sensible worlds. This, again, generated the particular souls, human, animal, and vegetive, and, lastly, all inorganic substances. The substratum of all

[1] Just so the Nominalists and their modern followers deny to reason a voice, not only on questions of pure ontology, but on all points settled by traditional dogma (Harnack, vi. 163); but thus to discard reason altogether is to make every superstition impregnable.

[2] The scholastic term was 'Actus purus,' pure actuality or energizing.

[3] The later history of the 'World-soul' is given in Renan's 'Averroes.' Dante censured it, and the Lateran Council of 1518 anathematized it. Pope, following Spinoza, revived it.

these manifestations of the One in the sensible world was matter, which was non-existent of itself (*mē on*), and yet the basis of each sensible object (*bathos ekastou*) ;[1] in other words, it was a mere potentiality of receiving the imprint of the Divine effluences.

The One, the Reason, and the World-soul, constitute the so-called Plotinian Trinity, which is one, not of equality, but of subordination. Plotinus says Reason (*Nous*) is the *Logos* of the One, and Soul (*Psychē*) the *Logos* of the Reason.[2]

So much for the theory. As regards practice Plotinus held that man's duty was to return to the One.[3] The motive for this return was the love of the divine spark in his soul for its source, and its consequent craving to be reunited therewith. The One was itself unmoved, but attracted its effluents through being the object of their love and desire. The return was to be effected by retracing the downward course into the realm of matter. By what Dionysius later called the 'negative way,' the mystic aspirant must abstract and strip off all the material and sensuous accretions which had overlaid his real essence. This was to be effected,[4] first, by practising civic virtues, next the purifying virtues of asceticism and self-mortification, and finally the deifying virtue of contemplation.[5] At last he would transcend all the barriers separating him from the One, and would be absorbed and reunited with the One. Of this blessed state he could only hope to gain transient glimpses during life, but when the body perished he would abide for ever one with the One. Plotinus sums up by saying this is 'the flight of the Alone to the Alone.'

As Dr. Bigg points out, this mystical ascent of the soul is

[1] 'Not-being' is an equivocal term—nothing in relation to God, but a very pernicious something in relation to man.

[2] Ennead,' V., 1 and 6, quoted in Whittaker's 'The Neoplatonists,' p. 37, note 1.

[3] Plotinus followed Plato, who had said man's object should be to attain likeness to God as far as possible (*Homoiōsis tō theō*).

[4] This threefold division of the virtues agrees with the Ṣūfī division of the Law, the Path, and the Truth.

[5] Contemplation, *Theōria* was *Theou orāsis*, the 'beholding God' according to the Schoolmen's derivation of the word. Plotinus says the One is seen 'in presence which is better than science' (*kata parousian epistēmēs kreittona*).

described by Augustine almost in the words of Plotinus:[1] 'Thus as we talked and yearned after the eternal life, we touched it for an instant with the whole force of our hearts. We said then, if the tumult of the flesh were hushed; hushed these shadows of earth, sea, and sky; hushed the heavens and the soul itself, so that it should pass beyond itself and not think of itself: if all dreams were hushed and all sensuous revelations, and every tongue and every symbol; if all that comes and goes were hushed—they all proclaim to him that hath an ear: "We made not ourselves; He made us who abideth for ever."—But suppose that, having delivered their message, they held their peace, turning their ear to Him who made them, and that He alone spoke, not by them, but for Himself, and that we heard His word, not by any fleshly tongue, nor by an angel's voice, nor in the thunder, nor in any similitude, but His voice, whom we love in these His creatures—suppose we heard Him without any intermediary at all—just now we reached out, and with one flash of thought touched the Eternal Wisdom that abides aboves all. Suppose this endured, and all other inferior modes of vision were taken away, and this alone were to ravish the beholder, and absorb him and plunge him in mystic joy, might not eternal life be like this moment of comprehension?'

This is an admirable statement of the Plotinian 'return' to the One.[2] It also well illustrates the main characteristic of the system—viz., its ultimate dependence on emotion rather than on intellect. Philosophy is only the handmaid of theology, only used to support and justify pre-existing beliefs. When his reason lands him in contradictions, as it must do when it tries to transcend its limits and outsoar the very

[1] See Bigg's 'Confessions of St. Augustine,' p. 321 and note. All these Plotinian ideas were worked into Christian theology by Clement and Origen, himself a pupil of Ammonius Saccas, under whom Plotinus had studied. See Bigg's 'Christian Platonists of Alexandria.'

[2] See Ghazzālī's account in Appendix III. Also ''Hayy Ibn Yokdhan' or 'Philosophus autodidactus,' published by Pococke in 1671, and now translated by Dr. Brönnle under the title 'The Awakening of the Soul' (Murray, 1905). See his Introduction, pp. 17-19. A passage of this is quoted by the Quaker Barclay in his 'Apology,' edition of 1678, p. 126. Plotinus's own account may be read in Thomas Taylor's translation (Bell and Son's reprint, 1895, pp. 301-324).

atmosphere that bears it up, Plotinus straightway falls back on feeling and the inner light. Love and faith are a mighty spell, as Jalāl-ud-dīn Rūmī says,[1] and with Plotinus love and faith are always at hand to supplement the deficiencies of pure intellect.

The best accounts of Plotinus are those of Harnack in his 'History of Dogma,' English translation, i. 347; of Caird in his 'Evolution of Theology in the Greek Philosophers,' ii. 210; and of Whittaker in his 'Neoplatonists.' Opinions differ as to whether he is to be classed as a Monist or as a Dualist. This would depend on whether his 'not-being' is to be regarded as nothing or as something. Be this as it may, no one can read his impassioned outpourings without seeing that his theological reasoned statements by no means give the full measure of his beliefs. What he did believe in with a very passion of conviction was a Deity endued in some sense with the principal attributes of a personal God.

[1] 'Masnavī,' p. 262.

APPENDIX III

GHAZZĀLĪ ON MYSTICAL UNION[1]

'PRAYERS[2] have three veils, whereof the first is prayers uttered only by the tongue; the second is when the mind, by hard endeavour and by firmest resolve, reaches a point at which, being untroubled by evil suggestions, it is able to concentrate itself on divine matters; the third veil is when the mind can with difficulty be diverted from dwelling on divine matters. But the marrow of prayer is seen when He who is invoked by prayer takes possession of the mind of him who prays, and the mind of the latter is absorbed in God whom he addresses, his prayers ceasing and no self-consciousness abiding in him, even to this extent that a mere thought about his prayers appears to him a veil and a hindrance. This state is called 'absorption' by the doctors of mystical lore, when a man is so utterly absorbed that he perceives nothing of his bodily members, nothing of what is passing without, nothing of what occurs to his mind—yea, when he is, as it were, absent from all these things whatsoever, journeying first *to* his Lord, then *in* his Lord. But if the thought occurs to him that he is totally absorbed, that is a blot; for only that absorption is worthy of the name which is unconscious of absorption.

'I know these words of mine will be called an insipid discourse by narrow theologians, but they are by no means devoid of sense. Why? The condition of which I speak is similar to the condition of the man who loves any other things —*e.g.*, wealth, honour, pleasures; and just as we see some

[1] The Arabic text and a Latin translation of this passage are given by Tholuck in his 'Ssufismus,' pp. 3 and 105.

[2] *Dhikr* is the term used to denote the orisons of the Dervishes.

engrossed by love, we see others overpowered by anger so that they do not hear one who speaks, or see one who passes, and are so absorbed by their overwhelming passion, that they are not even conscious of being thus absorbed. For so far as you attend to the absorption of your mind, you must necessarily be diverted from Him who is the cause of your absorption. . . .'

.'And now, being well instructed as to the nature of "absorption," and casting aside doubts, do not brand as false what you are unable to comprehend. God most high saith in the Koran: "They brand as false what they do not comprehend." The meaning of "absorption" having been made clear, you must know that the beginning of the path is the journey *to* God, and that the journey *in* God is its goal, for in this latter, absorption in God takes place. At the outset this glides by like a flash of light, barely striking the eye; but thereafter becoming habitual, it lifts the mind into a higher world, wherein the most pure, essential Reality is manifested, and the human mind is imbued with the form of the spiritual world whilst the majesty of the Deity evolves and discloses itself. Now, what first appears is the substance of angels, spirits, prophets, and saints, for a while under the veil of I know not what beautiful forms, wherefrom certain particular verities are disclosed; but by degrees, as the way is opened out, the Divine Verity begins to uncover His face. Can anyone, I ask, who attains a glimpse of such visions, wherefrom he returns to the lower world disgusted with the vileness of all earthly things, fail to marvel at those who, resting content with the deceits of the world, never strive to ascend to sublimer heights?'

جامی تن زن سخن طرازی تا چند
اظهار حقایق بسخن هست خیال
افسون گری و فسانه سازی تا چند
ای ساده دل این خیال بازی تا چند

در ژنده فقر عیب پوشی بهتر
چون بر رخ مقصود نقابست سخن
در نکته عشق تیز هوشی بهتر
از گفت و شنید ما خموشی بهتر

تا کی چو درای کردن افغان و خروش
گنجینه دریای حقایق نشوی
یکدم شو ازین هرزه درایی خاموش
تا دام که چون صدف نگردی همه گوش

ای گر [illegible] بدین
چون لال توان بود در و گر بس ازین
[illegible]
لب بگشای به نطق خاکت بدهان

تمت الرساله بعون الله
وحسن توفیقه وصلی الله
علی محمد و علی
آله وصحبه وسلم

ثانیست زیرا که مترتب نمیشود بر تجلی ثانی الا اضافهٔ وجود بر
اعیان و اظهار آنچه اندراج یافته بود در ایشان بمقتضی تجلی اول

بشنو سخنی مشکل و سری مغلق	هر فعل و صفت که شد باعیان ملحق
از یک جهت آن جمله مضافست بما	وز وجه دگر جمله مضافست بحق

چون مقصود ازین عبارت و مطلوب ازین
اشارت تنبیه بود بر احاطهٔ ذات حق سبحانه و تعالی و سریان
نور او در جمیع مراتب وجود تا سالکان آگاه و طالبان صاحب
انتباه بشهود هیچ ذات از مشاهدهٔ جمال ذات غافل
نشوند و بظهور هیچ صفت از مطالعهٔ کمالات صفات
غافل نگردند و آنچه مذکور شد در ادای این مقصود کافی
بود و به بیان این مطلوب وافی لاجرم بدین قدر اقتصار
افتاد و برین حیثیت رباعی اختصار کرده شد

و در ضمن فعلی و انفعالی عین فعلی و انفعالی و در ضمن علم ذوقی و وجدانی
عین علم ذوقی و وجدانی تا غایتی که در ضمن علم موجوداتی که بحسب
عرف ایشان را عالم نمیدانند عین علمیست که لایق حال ایشانست
و علی هذا القیاس سایر الصفات و الکمالات

هستی بصفاتی که در او بود نهان   دارد سریان در همه عین اعیان
هر وصف زغیبی که بود قابل آن   بر قد قبول عین گشتست عیان

ای ذات تو در ذوات اعیان ساری   اوصاف تو در صفاتشان متواری
وصف تو چو ذات مطلقست اما هست   در ضمن مظاهر از تقید عاری

کلام شیخ رضی الله عنه در بعضی مواضع فصوص
مشعر بآنست که وجود اعیان ممکنات و کمالات تابعه
مر وجود را بحق سبحانه و تعالی باعتبار مجموع تجلیین است
و اضافه وجود بحق و اضافه توابع آن باعیان باعتبار کلی

الرابعة للوجود في الموجودات باسرها

هستی بصفاتی که درو بود نهان	دارد سریان در همه اعیان جهان
هر وصف ز عینی که بود قابل آن	بر قدر قبول عین گشتست عیان ٦

همچنانک حقیقت هستی از جهت صرافت اطلاق خودش ساریست در ذوات جمیع موجودات بحیثیتی که دران ذوات عین آن ذواتست چنانکه آن ذوات در وی عین بوذند همچنین صفات کامله او وکلیّتها و اطلاقها در جمیع صفات موجودات ساری اند بمثابه که در ضمن صفات ایشان عین صفات ایشانند چنانکه صفات ایشان در عین آن صفات کامله عین آن صفات کامله بوذند مثلا صفت علم در ضمن علم عالم بجزویات عین علم بجزویاتست و در ضمن علم عالم بکلیات عین علم بکلیات

اما علم بر دو وجه است یکی آنکه بحسب عرف آنرا علم میگویند دیگر

آنکه بحسب عرف آنرا علم نمیگویند و هر دو قسم پیش ارباب

حقیقت از مقوله علم است زیرا که ایشان مشاهده میکنند

سرایت علم ذاتی حق را سبحانه در جمیع موجودات و از

قبیل قسم ثانی آنست مثلا که بحسب عرف آب را عالم نمیدارند

اما می‌بینیم او را که تمیز میکند میان بلندی و پستی از بلندی عدول

میکند و بجانب پستی جاری میگردد و همچنین در داخل جسم متخلخل

نفوذ میکند و ظاهر جسم متکاثف را ترطیب میکند و میگذرد

الی غیر ذلک پس از خاصیت علم است جریان وی بر

مقتضای قابلیت قابل و عدم مخالفت با آن اما درین

مرتبه علم در صورت طبیعت ظاهر شده است و علی هذا القیاس

سرایة العلم فی سایر الموجودات بل سرایة جمیع الکمالات

و تفاوت علم بحسب تفاوت حقایق در قبول نه
وجود کمالا و نقصانا پس آنچه قابلست مر وجود را علی الوجه
الاتم الاکمل قابلست مر علم را علی هذا الوجه و آنچه قابلست
مر وجود را علی الوجه الانقص نیز چنینست علی هذا الوجه و منشاء
این تفاوت غالبیت و مغلوبیت احکام وجوب
و امکانست در هر حقیقت که احکام وجوب غالبتر آنجا وجود
و علم کاملتر و در هر حقیقت که احکام امکان غالبتر وجود و
علم ناقصتر و غالبا که خصوصیت حکم تابعیت علم مر وجود را
که در کلام شیخ واقعست بر سبیل تمثیل است و الا جمیع
کمالات تابعه مر وجود را چون حیوة و قدرت و ارادت
و غیرها همین حالست و قال بعضهم قدس الله تعالی
اسرارهم هیچ فرد از موجودات از صفت علم عاری

از این جهت گرمیست از کیفیات زیرا که او از این
جهت کمالیست از کمالات بلکه از آن جهت که عیب
شده است مر عدم وصول ثمار را بکمالات لائقهٔ خود را
وهمچنین قتل مثلا که شریست شریت او نه از جهت قدرت
قاتلست بر قتل یا قاطعیت آلت یا قابلیت عضو مقتول
مر قطع را بلکه از جهت زوال حیاتست و آن امریست
عدمی الی غیر ذلک من الامثله

میدان بیقین که محض خیریست ای دل		هر جا که وجود کرده سیریست ای دل
پس شر همه مقتضای غیریست ای دل		هر شر ز عدم بود عدم غیر وجود

شیخ صدرالدین قونوی قدس الله تعالی سره
در کتاب نصوص میفرماید که علم تابعست مر وجود را
بان معنی که هر حقیقت از حقایق را که وجودیست علم

چون صفات و احوال و افعال که در مظاهر ظاهر است
فی الحقیقه مضاف بحق ظاهر در ان مظاهر است پس اگر احیانا
در بعضی از انها شری و نقصانی واقع باشد از جهة عدمیت
امری دیگر تواند بود زیرا که وجود من حیث هو وجود خیر
محض است و از هر امری وجودی که شری متوهم میشود
بواسطه عدمیت امر وجودی دیگر است نه بواسطه ان
امر وجودی من حیث هو امر وجودی

هر نعت که از قبیل خیر است و کمال	باشد ز نعوت ذات پاک متعال
هر وصف که در حساب شر است و وبال	دارد بقصور قابلیات مآل

حکما در انکه وجود خیر محض است دعوی ضرورت
کرده اند و از برای توضیح مثالی چند آورده اند و گفته که
برد مثلا متلف ثمار است و شر است نسبت با ثمار و نه

فی الحقیقة از حق ظاهر در ان مظاهر ظاهر پس نه از مظاهر

شیخ رضی الله عنه در حکمت علیه میفرماید لا فعل للعین بل

یفعل لربها فیها فاطمأنت العین ان یضاف الیها

پس نسبت فعل به بنده از جهة ظهور حقست بصورت او نه

نه از جهت نفس او   میخوان و وجود

و قدرت و فعل خود را از حضرت بیچون میدان

از ما همه عجز و نیستی مطلوبست
هستی و توابعش زما مسلوبست

این اوست پدید آمده در صورت ما
این قدرت و فعل از آن بما منسوبست

چون ذات تو منفی بود ای صاحب هش
از نسبت افعال بخود باش خمش

شیرین سخنی شنو مکن روی ترش
ثبت للعرش اولاً ثم انقش

وصافی خود برغم حاسد تا کی
ترویج چنین متاع کاسد تا کی

تو معدومی خیال هستی از تو
فاسد باشد خیال فاسد تا کی

آنچه موجود و مشهود است حقیقت وجود است اما باعتبار
تلبس باحکام و آثار اعیان نه از حیثیت تجرد از آنها زیرا که این
حیثیت بطون و خفا از لوازم اوست پس فی الحقیقه حقیقت
وجود همچنان بر حقیقت خود است بر وحدت حقیقی خود
که ازلاً بود و ابداً خواهد بود اما بنظر اغیار بسبب احتجاب
بصورت کثرت احکام و آثار متقید و متعین
در می آید و متعدد و متکثر می نماید

بحر است وجود جاودان موج زنان — زان بحر ندیده غیر موج اهل جهان
از باطن بحر موج بین گشته عیان — بر ظاهر بحر بحر در موج نهان

هستی که بود ذات خداوند عزیز — اشیا همه در وی اند و وی در همه نیز
اینست بیان آنکه عارف گوید — باشد همه چیز مندرج در همه چیز

هر قدرت و فعل که ظاهر از مظاهر صادر می نماید

تحقیق معانی از عبارات مجوی
بی رفع قیود و اعتبارات مجوی
خواهی یابی ز علت جهل شفا
قانون نجات از اشارات مجوی

گشتی بوقوف بر مواقف قانع
شد قصد مقاصدت ز مقصد مانع
هرگز نشود تا نکنی رفع حجب
انوار حقیقت از مطالع طالع

در رفع حجب کوش نه در جمع کتب
کز جمع کتب نمیشود رفع حجب
در طی کتب کجا بود نشاه حب
طی کن همه را و عد الی الله و تب

عظیم ترین حجابی و کثیف ترین نقابی جمال وحدت حقیقی را انتساب و تعددایست که در ظاهر وجود واقع شده است بواسطه تلبس آن باحکام و آثار و اعیان ثابته در حضرت علم که باطن وجود است و محجوبان را چنان می نماید که اعیان موجود شده در خارج و حال آنکه بوئی از وجود خارجی بمشام ایشان نرسیده است و همیشه بر عدمیت خود بوده اند و خواهند بود

مر این اعراض را وآنکه ارباب نظر میگویند که امثال

این مفهومات فصول نمیشود بلکه لوازم فصولند که بآن از

فصول تعبیر میکنند بواسطهٔ عدم قدرت بر فصول تعبیر

از حقایق فصول بر وجهی که ممتاز شوند از ماعدای خود تعبیر این

لوازم یا لوازمی که ازینها اخص باشد مقدمه ایست ممنوع و

کلامیست نامسموع و بر تقدیر تسلیم هرچه نظر با جوهر ذاتی

باشد قیاس بآن عین واحد عرضی خواهد بود زیراکه اگرچه ذاتیت

در حقیقت خارجست ازان عین واحد و قایمست با وجود

آنکه اینجا امری هست جوهری ورای عین واحد در غایت

بسیطیت تخصیص وقفی که کشف ارباب حقیقت که مقتبس است

از مشکوة نبوت بخلاف آن گواهی دهد و مخالف

عاجز باشد از اقامت دلیل

در هر آنی حقیقت عالم را   یک اسم فنا یکی بقا می‌بخشد

یل بر آنکه مجموع اعراض مجتمعه است در عین واحد که حقیقة
وجود است آنکه هر چند حقایق موجودات آنکه را تحدید میکنند
در حدود ایشان غیر از اعراض چیزی ظاهر نمیشود مثلا
که گویند انسان حیوان ناطق است و حیوان جسم نامی حساس
متحرک بالاراده و جسم جوهر قابل مر ابعاد ثلثه و جوهر موجود است
لا فی موضوع و موجود ذاتیست که مر او را تحقق و حصول
باشد درین حدود هر چه مذکور میشود از قبیل اعراض است
الا آن ذات مبهم که درین مفهومات ملحوظ است زیرا که
معنی ناطق ذات له النطق است و معنی نامی ذات
له النمو و هکذا فی البواقی و این ذات مبهم عین وجود
حق و هستی حقیقی است که قائمست بذات خود و مقومست

مقتضی اضمحلال تعینات و آثار کثرت صوری است ازان تعین منسلخ گردد و در همان آن انسلاخ بمقتضای رحمت رحمانیه تعینی دیگر خاص که مماثل تعین سابق باشد متعین گردد و در آن ثانی بقهر احدیت مضمحل گردد و تعینی دیگر برحمت رحمانیه حاصل و هکذا الی ما شاء الله پس در هیچ دو آن یک تجلی واقع نشود و در هر آنی عالمی بعدم رود و دیگری مثل آن بوجود آید اما محجوب بجهت تعاقب امثال و تناسب احوال می پندارد که وجود عالم بر یک حالست و در ازمنهٔ متوالیه بر یک منوال

سبحان الله زهی خداوند ودود | مستجمع کرم و فضل و رحمت و جود
در هر نفسی برد جهانی بعدم | و آرد دگری چو آن همان دم بوجود
انواع عطا گرچه خدا می بخشد | هر اسم عطیه جدا می بخشد

در هر نفسی متجلیست بتجلی دیگر و در تجلی او اصلا تکرار نیست یعنی
در دو آن بیک تعین و یک شان متجلی نمیگردد بلکه در هر نفسی
بتعین دیگر ظاهر میشود و در هر آنی بشانی دیگر متجلی میگردد

هستی که عیان نیست دو آن در شانی	در شان دگر جلوه کند هر آنی
این نکته بجو ز کل یوم هو فی شان	گر بایدت از کلام حق برهانی

و سر در این آنست که حضرت حق را اسماست متقابله
بعضی لطیفه و بعضی قهریه و همه دایما بر کارند و تعطیل بر هیچ
یک جایز نیست پس چون حقیقتی از حقایق امکانیه بواسطه حصول
شرایط و ارتفاع موانع مستعد وجود گردد رحمت رحمانیه
او را دریابد و بروی افاضه وجود کند و ظاهر وجود بواسطه
تلبس آثار و احکام آن حقیقت متعین گردد بتعینی خاص و
متجلی شود بحسب آن تعین بعد از آن بسبب قهر احدیت حقیقی که

بحریست نه کاهنده نه افزاینده ‌‌ امواج برو روند و آینده

عالم چو عبارت از همین امواج است ‌‌ نبود دو زمان بلکه دو آن پاینده

عالم بود ار نه ز عبرت عاری ‌‌ جهری جاری بطورهای طاری

وندر همه طورهای جهر جاری ‌‌ سریست حقیقة الحقائق ساری

و اما خطاء سوفسطائیه آنست که مع قولهم بالتبدل فی العالم
باسره متنبه نشده اند بآنکه یک حقیقت که متلبس میشود
بصور و اعراض عالم و موجودات متعینه متعدده می نماید
و ظهورات او را در مراتب کونی جز باین صور
و اعراض خیالیه وجودی نیست در خارج بدون او

سوفسطایی که از خرد بیخبرست ‌‌ گوید عالم خیالی اندر گذرست

آری عالم همه خیالست ولی ‌‌ پیوسته درو حقیقتی جلوه گرست

و اما ارباب کشف و شهود می بینند که حضرت حق سبحانه و تعالی

لا یبقی زمانین و مگر حسبانیه که معروفند بسوفسطائیه در همه اجزای
عالم چه جواهر و چه اعراض و هر یک از فریقین من وجهی
خطا کرده اند اما اشاعره بسبب آنکه اثبات جواهر متعدده
کرده اند ورای حقیقت وجود و اعراض متبدله متجدده
را بآنها قایم داشته و ندانسته اند که عالم بجمیع اجزاء
نیست مگر اعراض متجدده متبدله مع الآنات پس که در
در عین واحد جمع شده اند و در هر آنی از این عین زایل
میشوند و امثال آنها بوی ملبس میگردند پس ناظر بواسطه
تعاقب امثال در غلط می افتد و می پندارد آن امر
واحد مستمر کما یقول الاشاعرة فی تعاقب الامثال علی
محل العرض من غیر خلو آن من شخص من العرض مماثل
للشخص الاول فیظن الناظر انها امر واحد مستمر

و آخریت از نسب و اعتبارات است هو الاول و الآخر و الظاهر و الباطن

بر شکل بتان رهزن عشاق حقیقت	لا بلکه عیان در همه آفاق حقیقت
چیزی که بود ز روی تقیید جهان	والله که همان ز روی اطلاق حقیقت
چون حق بتفاصیل شیون گشت عیان	مشهود شد این عالم پر سود و زیان
گر باز رود عالم و عالمیان	با رتبهٔ اجمال حق آید بمیان

شیخ رضی الله عنه در فص شعیبی میفرماید که عالم عبارتست از اعراض مجتمعه در عین واحد که حقیقت هستی است و آن متبدل و متجدد میگردد مع الآنات و الانفاس در هر آنی عالم بعدم میرود و مثل آن بوجود می آید و اکثر اهل عالم ازین معنی غافلند کما قال سبحانه

و از ارباب نظر کسی برین مطلع نشده است

مگر اشاعره در اجزای عالم که اعراض است حیث قالوا الاعراض

همه اشیاست و او فی حد ذاته واحدیست که عدد را باو راه
نیست اما باعتبار تجلیات متکثره و تعینات متعدده در
مراتب تاگرته حقایق جوهریه متنوعه است و تابع آن حقایق
عرضیه تابعه پس ذات واحد بواسطه تعدد جواهر و اعراض
متکثره می نماید و من حیث الحقیقه یکیست که اصلا متعدد و متکثر نیست

ای بر سر حرف این و آن باز ده خط — پندار دویی دلیل بعدیست و سخط
در جمله کاینات بی سهو و غلط — یک عین مجرد دان و یک ذات فقط

این عین واحد از حیثیت تجرد و اطلاق از تعینات و تقیدات
مذکوره حقست و از حیثیت تعدد و تکثری که بواسطه تلبس
او بتعینات می نماید خلق و عالم پس عالم ظاهر حقست و حق
باطن عالم عالم پیش از ظهور عین حق بود و حق بعد از ظهور
عین عالم بلکه فی الحقیقه یک حقیقت و ظهور و بطون و اولیت

بس نت و اعیان حقایق بصور خود بر اوست

فی الحقیقه وجود یکی بیش نیست که در جمیع این مراتب و حقایق متمرتبه دران ساریست و وی درین مراتب و حقایق عین این مراتب و حقایقست چنانکه این مراتب و حقایق در وی عین وی بودند حیث

هستی که ظهور مى‌کند در همه شیء ‌ ‌ خواهی که بری بحال وی با همه پی

رو بر سر می حباب را بین که چه سان ‌ ‌ می وی بود اندر وی و وی در می

بر لوح عدم لوایح نور قدم ‌ ‌ لایح را دید و کس درین سر محرم

حق را مشمر جدا از عالم زیرا که		عالم در حق حقست و حق در عالم
	جز عالم نیست	

حقیقه الحقایق که ذات الهی است تعالی شانه حقیت

مرتبه ثانیه تعین اوست تعین جامع مر جمیع تعینات فعلیه وجوبیه
الهیه را و جمیع تعینات انفعالیه امکانیه کونیه را و این مرتبه مسماست
بتعین اول زیرا که اول تعینات حقیقت وجود اوست و فوق
او مرتبه لاتعینست لا مرتبه غیر ثالثه احدیت جمع جمیع تعینات
فعلیه مؤثره است و این مرتبه الوهیت مرتبه رابعه تفصیل
مرتبه الوهیتست و مرتبه اسما و حضرت ایشانست و اعتبار
این دو مرتبه از حیثیت ظاهر وجودست که وجوب وصف
خاص اوست مرتبه خامسه احدیت جمع جمیع تعینات
انفعالیه است که از شان ایشانست تأثر و انفعال و این
مرتبه کونیه امکانیه است مرتبه سادسه تفصیل مرتبه کونیه
امکانیه است که مرتبه عالم است و عروض این دو مرتبه
باعتبار ظاهر علمست که امکان از لوازم اوست و آن

وصفات و مقدس است از دلالت الفاظ و لغت
نه نقل را در نعت جلال او زبان عبارتست و نه عقل را امکان
کمال و مکان اشارت هم ارباب کشف از ادراک
حقیقتش در حجاب و هم اصحاب علم از استماع معرفتش
در اضطراب غایت نشان از وی بی‌نشانیست و
نهایت عرفان وی حیرانی

ای در تو عیانها و نهانها همه هیچ
پندار یقینها و گمانها همه هیچ

از ذات تو مطلقا نشان نتوان داد
کانجا که تویی بود نشانها همه هیچ

هرچند که جان عارف آگاه بود
کی در حرم قدس تواش راه بود

دست همه اهل کشف و ارباب شهود
از دامن ادراک تو کوتاه بود

این عشق که هست جزو لاینفک ما
حاشا که شود بعقل ما مدرک ما

خوش آنکه ز نور او دمد صبح یقین
ما را برهاند از ظلام شک ما

ونسب و اعتبارات مخصوصه است که در سایر مراتب نیست چون مرتبه الوهیت و ربوبیت و مرتبه عبودیت و ظلیت پس اطلاق اسامی مرتبه الهیت مثلا چون الله و رحمن و غیرها بر مراتب کونیه عین کفر و محض زندقه باشد و همچنین اطلاق اسامی مخصوصه بمراتب کونیه بر مرتبه الهیت غایت ضلال و نهایت خذلان باشد

ای برده گمان که صاحب تحقیقی | وندر صفت صدق و یقین صدیقی
هر مرتبه از وجود حکمی دارد | گر حفظ مراتب نکنی زندیقی

موجود حقیقی یکی بیش نیست و آن عین وجود حق و هستی مطلق است اما او را مراتب بسیار است اول مرتبه لاتعین و عدم انحصار است و اطلاق از هر قید و اعتبار از این حیثیت منزه است از اضافت نعوت

تعیّن بهمان شان در همان حضرت واشیاء موجوده

عبارت اند از تعینات وجود باعتبار انصباغ ظاهر

وجود با ثار و احکام حقایق ایشان یا خود وجود متعین

بهمین اعتبارات بر وجهی که حقایق همیشه در باطن وجود

پنهان باشند و احکام و آثار ایشان در ظاهر وجود پیدا

زیرا که زوال صور علمیه از باطن وجود محالست والا

جهل لازم اید

با همه وجوه و اعتبارات وجود

در خارج و در علم عارض ذات بود

ور پرتو ظلمت عدم مستوریم

ظاهر شده عکس از مرآت وجود

حقیقت وجود اگر بر جمیع موجودات ذهنی

و خارجی مقول و محمول میشود اما او را مراتب متفاوتست

و در هر مرتبه او را اسامی و صفات

هر کس که نباشد تو عوض باشی ازو / وانرا که نباشی تو کسی نیست عوض

استغنای مطلق از مقید باعتبار ذاتست والا ظهور اسماء الوهیت و تحقق نسب ربوبیت بی مقید از محالاتست

ای باعث شوق و طلبم خوبی تو / فرع طلب منست مطلوبی تو
گر آینهٔ محبتی من نبود / ظاهر نشود جمال محبوبی تو

لا بلکه هم محب حقیقت و هم محبوب او و هم طالب حقیقت و هم مطلوب او و مطلوبیت و محبوبیت در مقام جمع احدیت و طالبیت و محبیت در مرتبه تفصیل و کثرت

ای غیر ترا بسوی تو پی سیری / خالی ز تو مسجدی و دیری نی
دیدم همه طالبان و مطلوبان را / آن جمله توئی و درمیان غیری نی

حقیقت هر شی تعین وجودیست در حضرت علم باعتبار شانی که آن شی مظهر اوست یا تو و وجود

مطلق بی مقید نباشد و مقید بی مطلق
صورت نه بندد اما مقید محتاج بمطلق و مطلق
مستغنی از مقید پس استلزام از طرفین و احتیاج از
یک طرف چنانکه میان حرکت ید و حرکت مفتاح که در ید است

ای در حرم قدس تو کس را جائی — عالم بتو پیدا و تو خود پیدائی
ما و تو ز هم جدا نه ایم اما هست — ما را بتو حاجت و ترا با ما نی

و ایضاً مطلق مستلزم مقیدیست از مقیدات علی سبیل
البدلیه نه مستلزم مقید مخصوص و چون مطلق را بدلی نیست
فلا احتیاج همه مقیدات اوست لا غیر

قرب تو باسباب و علل نتوان یافت — بی سابقه فضل ازل نتوان یافت
از هر که بود توان گرفتن بدلی — تو بی بدلی ترا بدل نتوان یافت
ای ذات رفیع تو نه جوهر نه عرض — فضل و کرمت نیست معلل بغرض

ظهور و خفای شئون و اعتبارات بسبب تلبس
بمظاهر وجود و عدم آن موجب تغیر حقیقت وجود و صفات
حقیقیهٔ او نیست بلکه مبتنی بر تبدل نسب و اضافاتست و آن
مقتضی تغیر در ذات نی اگر عمرو از یمین زید برخیزد و بر
یسارش نشیند نسبت زید با او مختلف نشود و ذاتش با
صفات حقیقیهٔ خود همچنان برقرار و همچنین حقیقت وجود
بواسطهٔ تلبس بامور شریفه زیادتی کمال نگیرد و بجهت
ظهور مظاهر خسیسه نقصان نپذیرد و نور آفتاب هر چند
بر پاک و پلید تابد هیچ تغیر به بساطت نوریت او راه نیابد
نه از مشک بوی گیرد و نه از گل رنگ و نه خار عار و نه از خاره ننگ

چون خور ز فروغ خود جهان آراید	بر پاک و پلید اگر بتابد شاید
نی نور وی از هیچ پلید آلاید	نی پاکی از هیچ پاک افزاید

مراد باندراج کثرت شئون در وحدت
ذات نه اندراج جزویت در کل یا اندراج مظروف
در ظرف بلکه مراد اندراج اوصاف و لوازمست در موصوف
و ملزوم چون اندراج نصفیت و ثلثیت و ربعیت و خمسیت
الی ما لانهایة له در ذات واحد عددی زیرا که این نسب
در وی مندرجند و اصلا ظهور ندارند مادام که تکرار
طعر در مراتب جزو اثنین و ثلثه و اربعه و خمسه واقع نشود
و ازینجا معلوم میشود که احاطه حق سبحانه و تعالی بجمیع
معیت ذاتیه همچو احاطه ملزومیت بلوازم نه همچون احاطه کل بجزو
یا ظرف بمظروف تعالی الله لا یلیق بجناب قدسه

در ذات حق اندراج شان معروفست / شان چون صفتست و ذات حق موصوفست
این قاعده یاد دار کانجا که خداست / نه جزو نه کل نه ظرف نه مظروفست

و خواه تعینات و تشخصات همه شئون الهی اند مندرج
و مندمج بودند در وحدت ذات اولا در مرتبهٔ علم بصورت
اعیان ثابته برآمدند و ثانیا در مرتبهٔ عین بواسطهٔ تلبس
احکام و آثار ایشان بظاهر وجود که مجلی آئینه است
مر باطن وجود را صورت اعیان خارجیه گرفتند پس نیست
در خارج الا حقیقت واحد که بواسطهٔ تلبس بشئون و صفات
متکثره و متعدد می نماید نسبت با آنان که در مضیق مراتب
محبوس اند و باحکام و آثار آن مقید

مجموعهٔ کون را بقانون سبق	کردیم تصفح و ورق بعد ورق
حقا که ندیدیم و نخواندیم درو	جز ذات حق و شئون ذاتیهٔ حق
تا چند حدیث جسم و ابعاد و جهات	تا کی سخن معدن و حیوان و نبات
یک ذات فقط بود محقق نه ذوات	این کثرت وهمی شئونست و صفات

را و آنچه با او در تحت جسم نامی مندرجست رفع کنی همه در جسم

نامی جمع شوند و چون ممیزات جسم نامی را و آنچه با او مندرجست

تحت الجسم رفع کنی همه در حقیقت جسم جمع شوند و چون

ممیزات جسم را و آنچه با او مندرجست تحت الجوهر اعنی

العقول و النفوس رفع کنی همه در حقیقت جوهر جمع شوند و چون

مابه الامتیاز ممکن و واجب را جوهر و عرض را رفع کنی

همه در تحت ممکن جمع شوند و چون مابه الامتیاز ممکن و واجب

را رفع کنی هر دو در موجود مطلق جمع شوند که عین حقیقت

وجود است و بذات خود موجود است نه بوجود زاید

بر ذات خود و وجوب صفت ظاهر اوست و امکان

صفت باطن او اعنی الاعیان الثابتة الحاصلة بتجلیه علی

نفسه متلبساً بالشئون و این ممیزات خواه فصول و خواص

وتشابه فی المراتب وازین حیثیت از وجود جمیع
موجودات مستغنیست کما قال سبحانه ان الله لغنی عن العالمین

دامان غنای عشق پاک آمد پاک ‌‌ زآلودگی نیاز با مشتی خاک
چون جلوه گر و نظارگی جمله خود است ‌‌ گر ما و تو در میان نباشیم چه باک

هر شان و صفت که منشی حق دارد ‌‌ در خود همه معلوم و محقق دارد
در ضمن مقیدات محتاج بحوبش ‌‌ از دیدن آن غنای مطلق دارد

واجب ز وجود نیک و بد مستغنیست ‌‌ واحد ز مراتب عدد مستغنیست
در خود همه را چو جاودان می بیند ‌‌ از دیدنشان برون ز خود مستغنیست

چون تشخصات و تعینات افراد و انواع
مندرجه تحت الحیوان را رفع کنی افراد هر نوعی در ذاتی
جمع شوند و چون ممیزات آن انواع را که فصول و خواص اند
رفع کنی همه در حقیقت حیوان جمع شوند و چون ممیزات حیوان

وشهادت چه در دینی و چه در آخرت و مقصود از این همه

تحقیق و ظهور کمال اسمائیست که کمال جلا و استجلاست کمال

جلا یعنی ظهور را و بحسب این اعتبارات و کمال یعنی استجلا

شهود او مر آنها بحسب همین اعتبارات و این ظهور و شهود

عیانی عینی چون ظهور و شهود مجمل در مفصل بخلاف کمال ذاتی که ظهور

ذاتیست مر نفس خود را از برای نفس خود بی اعتبار غیر

و غیریت و این ظهوریست علمی غیبی چون ظهور مفصل در مجمل

و غنای مطلق لازم کمال ذاتیست و معنی غنای مطلق آنست که

شئون و احوال و اعتبارات ذات با احکامها و لوازمها

علی وجه کلی جملگی که در جمله مراتب حقایق الهی و کونی

می نماید مر ذات را از بطونها و اندراج الکل فی وحدتها

مشاهد و ثابت باشند بجمیع صورها و احکامها کما ظهرت و ثبتت

از وصور متفاوت ذات متلبسه بهذه الاعتبا
حقایق کونیه است و تلبس ظاهر وجود باحکام و آثار آنها
موجب تعدد وجودیست و بعضی ازان حقایق کونیه را
عند سریان الوجود فیها باحدیة جمع شئونه وظهور آثارها
واحکامها به استعداد ظهور جمیع اسماء و آیات سوی
الوجوب الذاتی علی اختلاف المراتب الظهور شده
وضعفا وغالبیة ومغلوبیة چون کمل افراد انسانی از انبیا
واولیا و بعضی را استعداد ظهور بعضیت دون بعضی
علی الاختلاف المذکور چون سایر موجودات و حضرت
ذات باحدیة جمع شئونها الالهیة والکونیه ازلا وابدا در جمیع
این حقایق که تفاصیل مرتبه واحدیه اند ساریست و متجلی
چه درعا ارواح و چه در عالم مثال و چه در عالم حس

بطون و اولیت و ازلیت و باعتبار اتصاف او بجمع
صفات و اعتبارات مرتبهٔ واحدیت و مراد از
ظهور و آخریت و ابدیت و اعتبارات مرتبهٔ واحدیت
بعضی از آن قبیلند که اتصاف ذات بآنها باعتبار مرتبه
جمعیت خواه مشروط باشند بتحقق وجود بعض حقایق
کونیه چون خالقیت و رازقیت و غیرهما و خواه نباشند
چون حیات و علم و ارادت و غیرها و اینها اسما و صفات الهیت
و ربوبیت اند و صورت معلومیت ذات متلبسه
بهذه الاسماء و الصفات حقایق الهیه است و ملتبس ظاهر
وجود بآنها موجب تعدد وجودی نیست و بعضی از آن قبیلند
که اتصاف ذات بآنها باعتبار مراتب کونیه است
چون فصول و خواص و تعینات که ممیزات اعیان خارجیه اند

ظاهر نوره و ظهر بالپس ستوره خفای او باعتبار صرافت
واطلاق ذاتیت و ظهور باعتبار مظاهر و تعینات

با گلرخ خویش گفتم ای غنچه دهان — هر لحظه مپوش چهره چون عشوه دهان
زد خنده که من بعکس خوبان جهان — در پرده عیان باشم و بی پرده نهان

رخسار تو بی نقاب دیدن نتوان — دیدار تو بی حجاب دیدن نتوان
ما دام که در کمال اشراق بود — سرچشمه آفتاب دیدن نتوان

خورشید چو بر فلک زند رایت نور — در پرتو او خیره شود دیده دور
و آندم که کند زیر پرده ابر ظهور — فالناظر تجلیه من غیر قصور

تعین اول وحدتیت صرف و قابلیت
محض مشتمل بر جمیع قابلیات چه قابلیت تجرد از جمیع اعتبارات
وصفات و چه اتصاف همه و باعتبار تجرد از جمیع اعتبارات
تا غایتی که از قابلیت این تجرد نیز مرتبه احدیت و مراوست

ذات من حیث هی از همه اسما و صفات معراست

و از جمیع نسب و اضافات مبرا اتصاف او باین امور

باعتبار توجه اوست بعالم ظهور در تجلی اول که خود بخود در خود

نمود نسبت علم و نور و وجود و شهود متحقق گشت ... و نسبت علم

و نسبت علم مقتضی عالمیت و معلومیت شد و نور مستلزم ظهور

و ظاهریت و مظهریت و وجود و شهود مستتبع واجدیت

و موجودیت و شاهدیت و مشهودیت و همچنین ظهور که

لازم نور است مسبوقست ببطون و بطون را تقدم ذاتی و

اولیتست ... نسبت با ظهور پس اسم اول و آخر و ظاهر و باطن

متعین شد همچنین در تجلی ثانی و ثالث الی ماشاء الله نسب

و اضافات متضاعف می شود و هر چند تضاعف نسب

و اسماء او بیشتر ظهور او بلکه خفاء او بیشتر فسبحان من احتجب

و اطلاق این اسم بر حضرت حق سبحانه بمعنی ثانی است نه بمعنی اول

هستی که قیاس عقل اصحاب بود | جز عارض اعیان حقایق نبود
زان پیش که کاشفات ارباب شهود | اعیان همه عارضند و معروض وجود

صفات غیر ذاتند من حیث المفهوم و المعقول و عین ذاتند من حیث التحقق و الحصول مثلا عالم ذات باعتبار صفت علم و قادر باعتبار قدرت و مرید باعتبار ارادت و شک نیست که اینها چنانکه بحسب مفهوم با یکدیگر متغایرند مر ذات را نیز مغایرند اما بحسب تحقق و هستی عین ذاتند باین معنی که آنجا وجودات متعدد نیست بلکه وجود یکیست واحد و اسما و صفات نسب و اعتبارات او

ای در همه شان ذات تو پاک از همه شین | نی در حق تو کیف توان گفت نه این
از روی تعقل همه غیرند صفات | با ذات تو وز روی تحقق همه عین

ذات همه جزو وجود قایم بوجود	ذات تو وجود ساذج و هستی بحت
بس بی رنگست یار دلخواه ای دل	قانع نشوی بزنـ[ـگ]ـها ای دل
اصل همه رنگها ازان بی رنگست	من احسن صبغة من الله ای دل

لفظ وجود را گاه بمعنی تحقق و حصول که معانی مصدریه و مفهومات اعتباریه اند اطلاق میکنند و بدان اعتبار از قبیل معقولات ثانیه است که در برابر وی امری نیست در خارج بلکه ماهیات را عارض میشود در تعقل چنانکه محققان حکما و متکلمین تحقیق آن کرده اند و گاه لفظ وجود گویند و حقیقتی میخواهند که هستی وی بذات خودست و هستی باقی موجودات بوی و فی الحقیقه غیر از وی موجودی نیست در خارج و باقی موجودات عارض ویند و قایم بوی چنانکه ذوق کمل کبراء عارفین و عظماء ا[illegible] محققین بآن گواهی میدهد

عمر جاودانی صرف آن نسبت کند هیچ نکرده باشد
و حق آن کما ینبغی بجای نیاورده

بر عود دلم نواخت یک زمزمه عشق | زان زمزمه ام ز پای تا سر همه عشق
حقا که بعهدها نیایم بیرون | از عهده حق گزاری یکدمه عشق

چیست حق سبحانه جز هستی نیست و هستی او را
انحطاط و پستی نی مقدس است از سمت تبدل و تغیر و مبرا است
از وصمت تعدد و تکثر از همه نشانها بی نشان نه در علم گنجد
و نه در عیان همه چیزها و چونها ازو پیدا و او بی چند
و چون همه چیزها با و مدرک و او از احاطه ادراک
بیرون چشم بصر در مشاهده جمال او خیره و دیده سرا
بینی ملاحظه کمال او تیره

یا من لهواه کنت بالروح سمحت | هم فوقی هم تحت نه فوقی و نه تحت

دوام این نسبت از وی دشوار است اما چون آثار جذبهٔ لطف در وی ظهور کند و مشغلهٔ محسوسات و معقولات را از باطن وی دور اندازد بآن غلبه کند بر لذات جسمانی و راحات روحانی کلفت مجاهده از میانه برخیزد و لذت مشاهده در جانش آویزد خاطر از مزاحمت اغیار بپردازد و زبان جانش بدین ترانه ترنم آغازد

کای بلبل جان مست بیاد تو مرا	وی مایهٔ غم پست زیاد تو مرا
لذات جهان را همه در پا فکنند	ذوقی که دهد دست زیاد تو مرا

چون طالب صادق مقدمهٔ نسبت جذبه را که التذاذ است بیاد کرد حق سبحانه در خود باز یابد میباید که تمامی همت را بر تربیت و تقویت آن گمارد و از هرچه منافی آنست خود را باز دارد و چنان داند که اگر فی المثل

از قبیل ماسوی حق سبحانه پس شعور بآن منافی فنا باشد

زینسان که بقای خویشتن میخواهی — از خرمن هستیت جوی کی کاهی
تا یکسر موز خویشتن آگاهی — گر دم زنی از ره فنا گمراهی

توحید یگانه گردانیدن دلست یعنی تخلیص و تجرید او از تعلق بماسوای حق سبحانه هم از روی طلب و ارادت و هم از جهت علم و معرفت یعنی طلب و ارادت او از همه مطلوبات و مرادات منقطع گردد و همه معلومات و معقولات از نظر بصیرت او مرتفع شود از همه روی توجه بگرداند و بغیر از حق سبحانه آگاهی و شعورش نماند

توحید بعرف صوفی ای صاحب سیر — تخلیص دل از توجه اوست بغیر
رمزی ز نهایات مقامات طیور — گفتم بتو گر فهم کنی منطق طیر

مادام که آدمی بدام هوا و هوس گرفتارست

آن نسبت قوی تر کوشش می باید کرد تا خواطر متفرقه از ساحت سینه خیمه بیرون زند و نور ظهور هستی حق سبحانه بر باطن پرتو افکند ترا از تو بستاند و از مزاحمت اغیار برهاند نه شعور بخودت ماند و نه شعور بعدم شعور بل لم یبق الا الله الواحد الاحد

یارب ز بدی گزیدی خود برهم
از بند بدم و ز بدی خود برهم
در هستی خود مرا ز خود بیخود کن
تا از خودی و بیخودی خود برهم

انرا که فنا شیوه و فقر آیین است
نی کشف و یقین نه معرفت نه دین است
رفت او ز میان همین خدا ماند خدا
الفقر اذا تم هو الله این است

فنا عبارت از انست که بواسطه استیلای ظهور هستی حق بر باطن بما سوای او شعور نماند و پوشیده نباشد که فنا فنا در فنا مندرجست زیرا که صاحب فنا را اگر بفنای خود شعور شد صاحب فنا نباشد بجهه آنکه صفت فنا و موصوف آن

در هیچ وقتی از اوقات و حالتی از حالات از آن نسبت خالی نباشی چه در آمدن و رفتن و چه در خوردن و خفتن و چه در شنیدن و گفتن و بالجمله در جمیع حرکات و سکنات حاضر وقت می باید بود تا بطالت نگذرد بلکه واقف نفس باشی تا بغفلت بر نیاید

رخ گرچه نمی نمائیم سال بسال — حاشا که بود مهر ترا وهم زوال
دارم همه جا باهمه کس در همه حال — در دل ز تو آرزو و در دیده خیال

همچنانکه امتداد نسبت مذکوره بحسب شمول جمیع اوقات و ازمان واجبست همچنین ازدیاد کیفیت آن بسبب تعری از ملابسه اکوان و تبری از ملاحظه صور امکان اهم مطالبست و آن جز بجهدی بلیغ و جدی تمام در نفی خواطر و اوهام میسر نگردد هر چند خواطر منتفی تر و وساوس مختفی تر

اقبال کنی و بحقیقتی اشتغال نمایی که درجات موجودات همه مجالی جمال اویند و مراتب کاینات مرایای کمال او و برین نسبت چندان مداومت نمایی که با جان تو درآمیزد و هستی تو از نظر تو برخیزد اگر بخود روی آوری روی باو آورده باشی و چون از خود تعبیر کنی تعبیر ازو کرده باشی مقید مطلق شود و انا الحق هو الحق

گر در دل تو گل گذرد گل باشی
ور بلبل بیقرار بلبل باشی
تو جزوی و حق کلست اگر روزی چند
اندیشهٔ کل پیشه کنی کل باشی

ز آمیزش جان و تن توئی مقصودم
وز مردن و زیستن توئی مقصودم
تو دیر بزی که من برفتم ز میان
گر من گویم ز من توئی مقصودم

کی باشد کی لباس هستی شده شق
تابان گشته جمال وجه مطلق
دل در سطوات نور او مستهلک
جان در غلبات شوق او مستغرق

و رزش این نسبت شریفه می باید کرد بر وجهی که

از هر طرفی جمال مطلق پیداست		ای بیخبر از چشم مقید چه کنی

آدمی اگرچه بسبب جسمانیت در غایت کثافتست

اما بحسب روحانیت در نهایت لطافتست بهرچه روی

آرد حکم ان گیرد و بهرچه توجه کند رنگ آن پذیرد ولهذا

حکما گفته اند چون نفس ناطقه بصور مطابق حقایق متحلی شود

و باحکام صادق آن متحقق گردد صارت کانها الوجود کله

و ایضا عموم خلایق بواسطه شدت اتصال بدین صورت

جسمانی و کمال اشتغال بدین پیکر هیولانی چنان شده اند که خود را

از ان باز نمی دانند و امتیاز نمی توانند وفی للمثنوی المولوی قدس سره

ای برادر تو همین اندیشهٔ		ما بقی تو استخوان و ریشهٔ
گر گلست اندیشهٔ تو گلشنی		ور بود خاری تو هیمهٔ گلخنی

پس باید که دیدهٔ خود را از نظر خویش و بر داری

جمیل سبحانه علی الاطلاق ذو الجلال و الافضالست

هر جمال و کمال که در جمیع مراتب ظاهر است پرتو جمال و کمال اوست آنجا تافته و ارباب مراتب بدان سمت جمال و صفت کمال یافته هر کرا دانایی دانی اثر دانایی اوست و هر کجا بینایی بینی ثمرهٔ بینایی اوست و بالجمله همه صفات اوست از اوج کلیت و اطلاق نزول فرموده و در حضیض جزویت و تقید تجلی نموده تا تو از جزو بکل راه بری و از تقید به اطلاق روی آوری نه آنکه جزو از کل ممتاز دانی و مقید از مطلق باز دانی

رفتم بتماشای گل آن شمع طراز چون دید میان گلشنم گفت بناز

من اصلم و گلهای چمن فرع منست از اصل چرا بفرع می‌مانی باز

از لطف قد و صباحت خد حکمی وز سلسلهٔ زلف مجعد حکمی

بدست آمال و امانی چه دهی و پشت اعتماد برین مزخرفات فانی چه نهی دل از همه برکن و در خدای بند و از همه بگسل و با خدای پیوند اوست که همیشه بود و همیشه باشد و چهرهٔ بقایش را غبار هیچ حادثه نخراشد

هر صورت دلکش که ترا روی نمود
خواهد فلکش ز زود در چشم ربود
تو دل بیکسی ده که در اطوار وجود
بودست همیشه با تو و خواهد بود

رفت آنکه بقبلهٔ بتان روی آرم
حرف غمشان بلوح دل بنگارم
آهنگ جمال جاودانی دارم
چشمی که نه جاودان از آن بیزارم

چیزی که نه روی در بقا باشد ابدا
آخر هدف تیر فنا باشی ازو
از هر چه بمرد کی جدا خواهی شد
آن به که بزندگی جدا باشی ازو

ای خواجه آمال و فرزند بدست
پیداست که مدت بقایش چند است
خوش آنکه دلش بدلبری دربند است
کش با دل و جان اهل دل پیوند است

حق سبحانه و تعالی همه جا حاضر است و در همه
حال بظاهر و باطن همه ناظر است زهی خسارت که تو
دیده از لقای او برداشته سوی دیگر نگری و
طریق رضای او بگذاشته راه دیگر سپری

آمد سحر آن دلبر خونین جگران
گفتا ای زتو بر خاطر من بار گران
شرمت بادا که من بسویت نگران
باشم تو نهی چشم بسوی دگران

ماییم براه عشق پویان همه عمر
وصل تو بجد و جهد جویان همه عمر
یک چشم زدن خیال تو پیش نظر
بهتر که جمال خوبرویان همه عمر

ما سوی حق عز و علا در معرض زوال است و فنا
حقیقتش معلومیت معدوم و صورتش موجودیت موهوم
دی روز نه بود داشت و نه نمود و امروز نمود است
بی بود و پیدا نیست که فردا از وی چه خواهد گشود زمام انقیاد

با امور متعدد پراگنده سازی و جمعیت آنکه از همه بمشاهدهٔ واحد پردازی. جمعی گمان برند که جمعیت در جمع اسباب است. در تفرقهٔ ابد ماندند فرقهٔ یقین دانستند که جمع اسباب از اسباب تفرقه است دست از همه افشاندند

ای در دل تو هزار مشکل ز همه
مشکل شود آسوده ترا دل ز همه
چون تفرقهٔ دلست حاصل ز همه
دل را بیکی سپار و بگسل ز همه

تا دام که در تفرقه و وسواسی
در مذهب اهل جمع شر الناسی
لاوالله ناهی نه نسناسی
نسناسی خود ز جهل می نشناسی

ای سالک ره سخن ز هر باب مگوی
جز راه وصول رب ارباب مپوی
چون علت تفرقه است اسباب جهان
جمعیت دل ز جمع اسباب مجوی

ای دل طلب کمال در مدرسه چند
اصول و حکمت و هندسه چند
هر فکر که جز ذکر خدا وسوسه است
شرمی ز خدا بدار این وسوسه چند

در عالم فقر بی نشانی اولی
در قصهٔ عشق بی زبانی اولی

زانکس که نه اهل ذوق و اسرار بود
گفتن ز طریق ترجمانی اولی

شعرم که دری چند چو روشن خردان
در ترجمهٔ حدیث عالی سندان

باشد ز من هیچ مدان معتمدان
این تحفه رسانند بشاه همدان

مَا جَعَلَ اللّٰهُ لِرَجُلٍ مِنْ قَلْبَيْنِ فِي جَوْفِهِ حضرت بیچون که ترا نعمت هستی داده است در درون تو جز یک دل نهاده است تا در محبت او یکروی باشی و یک دل و از غیر او معرض و برو مقبل نه آنکه یک دل را بصد پاره کنی و هر پاره را در پی مقصدی آواره کنی

ای آنکه بقبله وفا روست ترا
بر مغز چرا حجاب شد پوست ترا

دل در پی این و آن نه نیکوست ترا
یک دل داری بس است یک دوست ترا

تفرقه عبارت از آنست که دل را بواسطهٔ تعلق

یارب برهانیم ز حرمان چه شود   راهی دهیم بکوی عرفان چه شود
بس گبر که از کرم مسلمان کردی   یک گبر دگر کنی مسلمان چه شود

یارب ز دو کون بی نیازم گردان   وز افسر فقر سرفرازم گردان
در راه طلب محرم رازم گردان   زان ره که نه سوی تست بازم گردان

این رساله ایست مسمّی بلوایح در بیان معارف ومعانی که بر الواح اسرار وارواح ارباب عرفان واصحاب ذوق و وجدان لایح گشته بعبارات لایقه واشارات رایقه متوقّع که وجود متصدّی این بیانرا درمیان نه بیند وبر بساط اعراض وسماط اعتراض ننشینند چه اورا درین گفت وگوی نصیبی جز منصب ترجمانی نی وبهره غیر از شیوه سخن رانی نی

من هیچم وکم ز هیچ هم بسیاری   از هیچ وکم از هیچ نیاید کاری
هر سر که ز اسرار حقیقت گویم   زانم نبود بهره بجز گفتاری

ما بگشای و هر چیز را چنانکه هست بما بنمای نیستی را بر ما در صورت هستی جلوه مده از نیستی بر جمال هستی پرده منه این صور خیالی را آئینه تجلیات جمال خود گردان نه علت حجاب و دوری و این نقوش وهمی را سرمایه دانایی و بینایی ما گردان نه آلت جهالت و کوری و محرومی و مهجوری ما همه از ماست ما را بما مگذار ما را از ما رهایی کرامت کن و با خود آشنایی ارزانی دار

یارب دل پاک و جان آگاهم ده	آه شب و گریه سحرگاهم ده
در راه خود اول ز خودم بیخود کن	آنگه بیخود ز خود به خود راهم ده

یارب همه خلق را بمن بدخو کن	وز جمله جهانیان مرا یکسو کن
روی دل من صرف کن از هر جهتی	در عشق خودم یک جهت و یک رو کن

ما را چه حد حمد و ثنای تو بود   هم حمد و ثنای تو سزای تو بود

جایی که زبان آور انا افصح علم فصاحت انداخته و خود را در ادای ثنای تو عاجز شناخته هر شکسته زبانی را چه امکان زبان گشایی و هر آشفته رایی را چه یارای سخن آرایی بلکه اینجا اظهار اعتراف بعجز و قصور عین قصور است و با آن سرور دین و دنیی درین معنی مشارکت جستن از حسن ادب دور

من کیستم اندر چه شمارم چه کسم   تا همسری سگانش باشد هوسم
در قافله که اوست دانم نرسم   این بس که رسد ز دور بانگ جرسم

اللهم صل علی محمد ناصب لواء الحمد و صاحب المقام المحمود و علی آله و اصحابه الفائزین بنیل المجهود و نیل المقصود و سلم تسلیما کثیرا

الهی الهی خلصنا عن الاشتغال بالملاهی و ارنا حقایق الاشیاء کما هی غشاوهٔ غفلت از بصر بصیرت

لا احصی ثناء علیک کیف وکل ثناء یعود الیک جل عن
ثنای جناب قدسک انت کما اثنیت علی نفسک خداوندا
سپاس تو بر زبان نمی آریم و ستایش تو بر تو نمی شماریم
هرچه در صحایف کاینات از جنس اثنیه و محامدست همه
بجناب عظمت و کبریای تو عاید است از دست و زبان
ما چه آید که سپاس و ستایش ترا شاید تو چنانی که خود
گفته و گوهر ثنای تو آنست که خود سفته

انجا که کمال کبریای تو بود
هستی نمی از بحر عطای تو بود

www.ingramcontent.com/pod-product-compliance
Ingram Content Group UK Ltd.
Pitfield, Milton Keynes, MK11 3LW, UK
UKHW021408190726
13845UKWH00028B/956